TEACHER RESOURCE BOOK 1–2

GRAMMAR RULES!

Second edition

Tanya Gibb

macmillan education

This edition published in 2016 by

macmillan education

MACMILLAN SCIENCE AND EDUCATION AUSTRALIA PTY LTD
15–19 Claremont Street, South Yarra 3141
Visit our website at www.macmillaneducation.com.au
Associated companies and representatives throughout the world.

First published in 2006.

Publisher: First edition Sharon Dalgleish
Designers: Trish Hayes and Stephen Michael King
Illustrator: Stephen Michael King

Printed in the UK at CLOC Book Print
MEA9_Nov17_02

Contents

Introduction

The *Grammar Rules!* Series

Grammar Rules! is an award-winning series of six student books and two Teacher Resource Books, which have been reproduced in a second edition. This second edition includes a disc in the Teacher Resource Books, Scope and Sequence charts updated for the Australian Curriculum and reflection activities in student books 1–4 to allow students to assess their own progress.

The *Grammar Rules!* series provides a context-based approach to grammar teaching and learning to ensure that students understand how to use their knowledge of grammar when constructing their own texts and responding to the texts of others. The series supports teaching and learning in English as described in the Language, Literature and Literacy Strands of the Australian Curriculum, English.

The sample texts and associated activities in the student books, as well as the supplementary activities suggested in the Teacher Resource Books, provide opportunities for students to develop the general capabilities of critical and creative thinking, personal and social capability, ethical understanding and intercultural understanding, as defined and described in the Australian Curriculum, English. Where possible, suggested activities also address ICT capabilities and cross-curriculum priorities.

Grammar Rules! shows students how grammatical structures and features function in texts to achieve meaning, from the contextual level of the whole text down to sentence and clause level and to the level of word groups, individual words and word parts. The series deals with the appropriate grammatical structures for particular types of texts, purposes for using language, and audiences.

The student books and Teacher Resource Books include **Scope and Sequence** charts. These charts give an overview of the whole program. They are also a useful index to the lessons and topics in each unit. Teachers can use the Grammar Program Checklists on **Reproducible 11** (page 85) and **Reproducible 12** (page 86) in their programs to keep track of the grammar concepts covered in class. The checklists are based on the Scope and Sequence charts in the *Grammar Rules!* student books. Teachers can use the Comment column to write their evaluation of any grammar activities undertaken with students and to note any follow-up activities required, or further comments.

The student books include 35 **units** of work for students to complete, including 6 Revision Units, which can be used for assessment purposes. Each unit focuses on one or more aspects of grammar, but the units also lend themselves to extension or enrichment with further aspects of grammar able to be explored if the teacher chooses or if students are ready, interested or in need of extension. Each unit builds upon knowledge gained in previous units.

The units cover a range of informative, imaginative and persuasive texts. Each individual unit in the student books is based on a **model text** that establishes the context for both the grammar focus of the unit and the grammar activities included in the unit. Teachers and students can explore the structure and meaning of each text before exploring the grammar in that context.

Each unit concludes with a **Try it yourself!** activity. This activity enables students to further extend their understanding of the type of text as well as demonstrate their knowledge of the grammar covered in the unit. The Try it yourself! refocuses students' attention on the influence of context and text on grammar choices.

Each *Grammar Rules!* student books includes a pull-out section with a Student **Writing Log**. The Writing Log provides a way for students to keep track of the types of texts and text forms they are writing, and the grammar they are attempting to use in the context of their writing. The Writing Logs support students' independence and encourage students to develop responsibility for their own writing tasks.

Footers at the end of each unit are cross-referenced with the Scope and Sequence charts. Along with the Scope and Sequence charts, they are a useful reference for teachers when programming or when looking for a particular grammatical concept.

What is Grammar?

Grammar is a system for organising language. It is a tool for making meaning and it is a body of knowledge in its own right. Grammar is essential for communicating effectively. It enables speakers and writers to get their message across to readers and listeners. It enables readers and listeners to interpret and analyse the way information and opinions are constructed to shape their view of the world. An understanding of the way grammar works in texts is important for effective language use across learning areas.

How to Develop a Whole-School Grammar Policy

On pages 6 and 7 you'll find a sample policy to use as a starting point to develop your own whole-school grammar policy. A whole-school policy could contain the following sections:

Philosophical Statement and Rationale
These statements explain why the school has decided to implement a whole-school policy; what the school values or believes about the teaching and learning of grammar; and how grammar is relevant to the particular learning needs of students enrolled in the school.

Aim/s
This should clearly articulate the overall aim/s of a whole-school approach to grammar.

Objectives
These are broad statements of the values and attitudes, skills and knowledge that are promoted by the school's policy.

Student Assessment
This part of the school's policy should clearly articulate the ways of collecting, recording, storing and using assessment information in the school. Assessment information can be cross-referenced to the Australian Curriculum and each state's syllabus documents.

Teaching Implications
These should cover:

- how grammar will be taught in each year group
- how grammar will be taught to the range of learners in the school
- how and when students will be assessed and how the assessment information will be reported to families
- the purchasing of resources and support materials
- teacher professional development and the training requirements of volunteers.

Evaluation
How will the policy be evaluated, by whom and in what time frame?
What will be done with the evaluation information? How, when and by whom will the policy be revised?

Grammaville State School

Whole-school Grammar Policy

Philosophy

The staff and families at Grammaville State School value the home languages and social dialects of students and families at the school and recognise that these provide effective means of communication in particular community situations. However, the staff and families at Grammaville State School believe that an understanding of the grammar of Standard Australian English will enable students to:

- create effective texts for a range of social purposes in the wider community
- analyse the texts constructed by others and understand the way language choices affect meaning
- learn more effectively across learning areas
- participate equitably in Australian society.

Rationale

A coherent, systematic teaching approach to grammar and different types of texts will ensure that students develop the knowledge and skills essential for effective communication in English and have fair and equitable access to opportunities beyond school, based on their ability to use Standard Australian English.

Aim

All students will be provided with systematic and sequential instruction in English grammar in the context of a range of informative, imaginative and persuasive texts, so that they:

- develop positive attitudes to learning in English
- experience success in creating a range of grammatically well-constructed texts to achieve social purposes (recount, inform, persuade, argue, explain, respond, describe, entertain, narrate, direct, instruct, discuss)
- use, appreciate, critically analyse and evaluate texts constructed by others.

Objectives

1. Students will value grammar and develop confidence in themselves as users of English.
2. Students will develop knowledge of language structures and features appropriate in different contexts for different purposes and audiences.
3. Students will use their knowledge of language structures and features in a range of texts in their own reading, writing, talking, listening and viewing.

Curriculum Links

See Australian Curriculum, English.

Refer to the Scope and Sequence charts from the *Grammar Rules!* Teacher Resource Books and student books.

Student Assessment

Information about student achievement in grammar will be collected spontaneously during class work and using a combination of students' writing samples and students' spoken texts.

Assessment information will also be collected on a regular and systematic basis using the Revision units provided in the *Grammar Rules!* student books as well as through specific tasks set for students, such as those in the student books' **Try it yourself!** sections.

Students will engage in self-assessment using the pull-out pages in their *Grammar Rules!* student books to record their use of different types of texts and grammar. Students can reflect on their progress in grammar within the context of their own writing, and record issues discussed in writing conferences held with the teacher.

Information about students' language achievements will be recorded and this information will be provided to families informally, as the need arises, and formally, in response to requests from families or as determined by the teacher.

Families will be provided with half-yearly and yearly written reports that outline grammar progress and development.

Teaching Implications

The school will implement this policy commencing Term 1 of ______ (year) in all classes.

Grammar instruction will be integrated across all areas of learning. Grammar instruction will be supported by the classroom expectation that all students will engage in writing and speaking, daily, for a variety of purposes and audiences.

Grammar instruction will be planned for daily, as well as occur spontaneously during the course of any activity that provides a teaching opportunity for grammar.

Support Material/Resources

Grammar Rules! resources will be purchased for each student and class teacher.

Whole-staff training and professional development opportunities in grammar will be organised.

Evaluation

Evaluation of the policy and policy review will be ongoing. Year-group meetings will be held monthly.

Year groups will provide written feedback to the Grammar Committee about the impact of this policy on students and staff.

The Grammar Committee will compile a written report for the school community on the progress of policy implementation and make further recommendations to school management regarding teacher training, resources (personnel and equipment), and so on.

<u>Key things to remember:</u>

- Integrate grammar across the curriculum.
- Teach grammar in context as it arises in students' own written and spoken texts and the texts students are using.
- Teach grammar by creating contexts for learning grammar.
- Teach grammar at the point of need for individual students as well as to the whole class, as appropriate, or to groups of students with similar needs.
- Consider ways to teach special groups such as ESL students.

Glossary

abstract noun
a noun for something that cannot be seen, heard or touched, such as an emotion or an idea *(love)*

adjective
a word that tells more about a **noun** or **pronoun** (see also **classifying adjective, describing/ descriptive adjective, number adjective**)

adverb
a word that adds meaning to a **verb** *(walk slowly)*, an **adjective** *(very pretty)* or another **adverb** *(really well)*. Adverbs can tell how *(quickly)*; when *(soon, now, then)*; where *(here, there, down)*.

alliteration
when words begin with the same sound *(slippery slugs)*

antonym
a word that means the opposite of another word *(clean/dirty)*

auxiliary verb
see **helping verb**

being or having verb
a being or having word *(is, has, was)*

classifying adjective
an adjective that classifies or tells the group that a **noun** belongs to *(gum tree)*

clause
a group of words that expresses an idea and contains a **verb** *(I caught the ball)*

collective noun
a name for a group of things *(herd, flock, pack)*

command
a sentence that tells someone to do something *(Finish your work.)*

common noun
an everyday naming word

comparative adjective
refers to both comparative and superlative adjectives, which are the forms of an adjective that show a degree of comparison (*dirtier* – comparative, *dirtiest* – superlative)

complex sentence
a sentence that has a main clause and one or more other clauses that add meaning to the main clause *(If the dog barks, the cat will run away.)*

compound sentence
a sentence containing more than one **clause**, where each clause makes sense on its own *(I will walk and she will drive.)*

compound word
a word made by combining two or more words *(everywhere, anybody, someone)*

concrete noun
a noun for something that can be seen, heard or touched

conjunction
a joining word that links words, **phrases** or **clauses** in a **sentence** *(and, but, because, so)*. Conjunctions are **connectives**.

connective
a word or words that connect ideas and events in a text by adding information *(and, as well as)*, comparing things *(on the other hand, alternatively)*, showing one thing causes another *(because, so)*, showing time sequence *(then, when, next)* or showing logical order *(firstly, finally)*

contraction
a shortened form of a word or words where letters are left out. An apostrophe shows that a letter or letters have been left out. *(I'm, what's)*

describing/descriptive adjective
an adjective that describes aspects of a noun such as its size, shape, texture and colour *(big round bumpy green frog)*

doing verb
a doing word that tells the action *(jump, eat, skip)*

ellipsis
when words have been left out of a sentence. Meaning is implied but not stated in words.

emotive word
a word that appeals to the emotions. Emotive words are often used in the media, in exposition texts *(the slaughter of whales)* and in advertising *(Don't miss out!)*.

evaluative language
language that represents the author's personal opinions and judgements about something *(delicious food, brave explorer)*

exclamation
a sentence that shows strong emotion, such as anger or surprise, or gives a warning or command. An **exclamation** ends in an exclamation mark. *(Wow! Look out! I love it!)*

helping verb
a **verb** that helps another verb *(is sleeping, was running)*, also called an auxiliary verb

homophone
a word that sounds the same as another word but is spelled differently and has a different meaning *(flour/flower)*

how word
an **adverb** that tells how to do something *(tread carefully, sing loudly)*. How words add meaning to verbs. (see also **adverb**)

joining word
see **connective**

lexical chain
see **word chain**

modality
the degree of certainty, usualness or obligation the speaker or writer has about something. **High modality** is certain; **low modality** is less certain. *(It will rain* – high; *It might rain* – low; *It won't rain* – high*)*

noun
a word for a person, place, animal or thing *(teacher, Australia, crocodile, desk)*

noun group
a group of words that contains a main **noun** and other words that tell more about the main noun *(the football field, my new red shoes)*

number adjective
an adjective in the **noun group** that tells the quantity or order of a noun *(every tree, some trees, five cakes, first term)*

onomatopoeia
when words sound like the things they represent *(whiz, clunk)*

paragraph
a sentence or a number of sentences based on the same idea. A paragraph begins on a new line.

personal pronoun
a **pronoun** that replaces a **noun** for a person, place, animal or thing. Personal pronouns can be 1st person *(I, me, we, us)*, 2nd person *(you)* or 3rd person *(her, him, she, he, them, they, it)*.

phrase
a group of words that go together to make meaning. A phrase usually does not include a **verb**. *(during the week, to the beach)*

plural noun
the form of the noun used for more than one person, place, animal or thing *(children, shops, birds, stitches)*

possessive adjective
a word in a noun group that shows ownership *(his hat)*

preposition
a word that shows the relationship between a **noun** or **pronoun** and another word *(on, in, under, below, around, through, with, by)*

prepositional phrase
a **preposition** linked to a **noun**, **pronoun** or **noun group**. A prepositional phrase can tell where *(under the old wooden bridge)*; when *(on Monday)*; how *(by a falling rock)*; or with whom *(with her)*.

pronoun
a word that can replace a **noun**

proper noun
a name for a particular person, place, animal or thing, beginning with a capital letter *(Timothy, Australia, Fido, Olympic Games)*

question
a **sentence** that asks for information or an opinion. A question ends in a question mark.

quoted speech
the actual speech someone says. Quoted speech needs speech marks (inverted commas). *("The excursion is on Wednesday," said the teacher.)*

reported speech
speech that is not quoted directly *(The teacher said that the excursion is on Wednesday.)*

rhyme
when the ends of words sound the same *(Humpty Dumpty)*

saying verb
a verb that shows something is being said *(yelled, whispered)*

sentence
a group of words that makes sense. A sentence must include at least one **verb**. Sentences end in full stops, question marks or exclamation marks.

simple sentence
a sentence that consists of a single **clause**

singular noun
the form of the noun used for a single person, place, animal or thing

speech marks
marks used to show words that are spoken in **quoted speech**, also called inverted commas or quotation marks

statement
a **sentence** that presents a fact or an opinion. A statement ends in a full stop.

superlative adjective
see **comparative adjective**

synonym
a word that has a similar meaning to another word *(small/little)*

tenor
refers to the roles and relationships of the people involved in the language situation

tense
refers to the ways in which time is represented in the forms of the verb. Tense is described as past *(I <u>ran</u> to school/I <u>was running</u> to school.)*; present *(I <u>am running</u> to school/I <u>run</u> to school)* and future *(I <u>will run</u> to school/I <u>intend to run</u> to school tomorrow)*.

theme
theme is the starting point of the message in the clause. It is the first grammatical component of the clause.

thinking or feeling verb
a verb that represents a mental activity *(I <u>love</u> cauliflower)*

time word
a word that helps sequence events in a text through time *(meanwhile, firstly, then, after, in the morning, next week, at 8 pm, this Tuesday)*. Time words can be **connectives**, **adverbs**, **prepositional phrases** or **noun groups**.

verb
a doing, being or having, thinking or feeling, or saying word

verb group
a group of words that does the job of a **verb**. It can contain a main verb and an auxiliary verb *(should try, is dancing)* or two verbs that contribute equally to the meaning (*remembered feeling* – this type is also known as a complex verb).

vocative
a name or title used to address a person and signal the nature of the relationship between the language users and their relative status *(Sir, Mum, Darling)*

word chain
a chain of words that represents a particular content strand in a text *(the old dog . . . yellow Labrador . . . family member)*. This is also called a lexical chain.

Displays

Organise classroom displays of a variety of texts to help raise students' awareness of differences between texts. Include examples of different types of texts across learning areas, including:

factual books related to class topics
picture books
play scripts
novellas
novels
poetry
magazines
advertising leaflets
business letters
informal letters

postcards
emails
travel brochures
diaries and journals
surveys
questionnaires
scientific explanations
comic strips
board games
song lyrics

Displays can include texts that are beyond the reading levels of students in the class. Students can explore visual elements in these texts or have the texts read to them. Diagrams, labels, charts, flow diagrams, cycle diagrams, graphs, timelines, illustrations and maps provide visual support to assist readers' understanding of texts. They can also be created by students as a demonstration of their understanding of a text.

Relate all grammar learning to the texts that are available in the school, home and community. For example, models of procedural texts could include: rules for maths games, rules for classroom behaviour, rules for sports, instructions for the tooth fairy about collecting teeth, directions to get to various parts of the school from the classroom, instructions for cleaning the class fish tank or caring for class plants, recipes for modelling clay or favourite family food treats, maps of the suburb or area, maps of the school grounds with routes marked in to various points, a plan of the classroom, a timetable for the day or week, a calendar of events for the year, a list of class jobs and a roster to show which students are responsible for which duties at any given time.

Display grammar definition posters, or create your own posters showing word banks (lexical chains) for topic lists, word banks for thinking and feeling verbs, verbs to use for 'saying' other than *said*, time connectives, prepositions, <u>how</u> adverbs, maps with proper nouns for place names, singular and plural nouns, contractions, adjectives for particular book characters or animals, and so on. Add to word banks as the school year progresses.

Display examples of students' written texts that show writing for a variety of social purposes, topics and audiences.

Provide different audiences for students' spoken texts – peers, other classes, small groups, whole-school assemblies, family members, invited guests such as senior citizens, imaginary guests, characters in literature and so on.

Make a 'what we did today' reflection chart or a 'what we did this week' reflection chart. It can be an A3-sized poster or a page of a scrapbook, initially written by the teacher with students' input but eventually written by pairs of students. It can be written towards the end of each day or week and displayed for family members and other students to read. It can include digital photos if the class has access to a printer and a camera, tablet or other device for taking photos. The reflection chart will include aspects of recount and response, with different types of verbs (doing/action, thinking and feeling, and so on). It should include a summary of the day's highlights or the week's events with personal comments.

Modelling and Demonstration

Demonstrate for students how to write different types of texts. Construct texts in front of the class or a particular group of students. Tell students what you are thinking as you write. For example, when demonstrating the construction of a recount, talk out loud about chronological sequence, time words and past tense. Articulate for students why you have included particular events, what is significant about them and therefore why they belong in the recount. Model how you think about your writing as you write. This shows students that writers change their minds, reorder things, cross out, consider different ways to write things, choose 'better' words and self-correct as they write.

Collaboratively create texts with students. For example, after a class excursion to a park, nature reserve or botanical gardens, jointly construct a description. Ask students to contribute adjectives to help describe what they have seen. Prompt them for figurative language such as simile by saying 'the trees looked like. . . '. Students might also suggest descriptions that are examples of personification or metaphor. Ask students for suggestions about connecting the ideas in the text in a logical sequence, which verb groups would be appropriate and so on.

Have students engage in collaborative language tasks in pairs or small groups where they discuss the purpose, structure and grammar of their texts. Collaborative and group work consolidates learning for those students who have learned particular aspects of grammar, and supports and extends those students who are still developing in that area. Students who are more capable or who are gifted in verbal-linguistic intelligence deserve opportunities to work on language tasks together or with students in other classes, otherwise they might resent always being teamed with less verbal-linguistically able students. Working in ability groups enables gifted students to extend and challenge each other.

In any group work, encourage students to articulate for each other the grammar choices they are making when they collaboratively construct texts. Model this when you demonstrate how to create particular texts for particular purposes.

Use published texts as models for innovation:

Jack and the Beanstalk → 'Jenny and the Beanstalk'

The Three Little Pigs and the Big Bad Wolf → 'The Three Mean Pigs and the Poor Little Wolf'

Ten in the Bed → 'Ten in the Boat'

We're going on a Bear Hunt → 'We're going on a Crocodile Hunt'.

Activities to Support Grammar Learning

CLOZE

Cloze involves deleting words or word groups from a text and asking students to use their knowledge of the way texts are structured and the grammar of texts to work out the missing words. When constructing cloze passages, make sure the text can still be read and makes sense. Keeping the first sentence intact is useful to help students establish the context. Some example cloze activities are included on **Reproducibles 1** and **2**. These have been created from text samples in Student Book 1. You could also read the cloze to students saying 'blank' where a word has been left out. Cloze works particularly well to identify students' understanding of word chains for reference (reference chains), lexical chains, articles, adjectives, verbs and verb tense. It is usually best to focus on one aspect of grammar only in each cloze activity. Students can complete cloze exercises either working independently or working in groups. Cloze passages are also a useful diagnostic tool for assessing grammar.

<u>Jigsaw cloze</u> involves cutting a text into chunks (paragraphs, sentences) and asking students to reassemble the pieces in the correct order. Jigsaw cloze works well to identify students' knowledge of text structures, particularly procedures (directions, instructions and recipes), recounts, expositions and information reports. An example jigsaw cloze text is included on **Reproducible 3**. This has been created from a text sample in Student Book 1. Cut along the dotted lines to divide the passage into separate sentences, and

have students reassemble the passage. **Reproducible 3** can also be used for <u>sentence cloze</u>. Sentence cloze involves cutting a sentence into individual words or word groups (grammatical parts). Students need to use knowledge of grammar to reassemble them. Sentence cloze is particularly useful for lower primary students and students learning English as a second language. <u>Oral cloze</u> involves the teacher reading to students (particularly narratives), pausing during the reading and asking for predictions about what might happen next. Students need to identify aspects of the text that enabled them to make their predictions.

Concept Maps and Semantic Webs

When students brainstorm ideas or prior knowledge about a topic it is useful to collate this knowledge in a structured format such as a concept map or semantic web. Concept maps and semantic webs are visual ways of organising and recording lexical words or content words – the key words related to a topic.

<u>Concept Map</u>

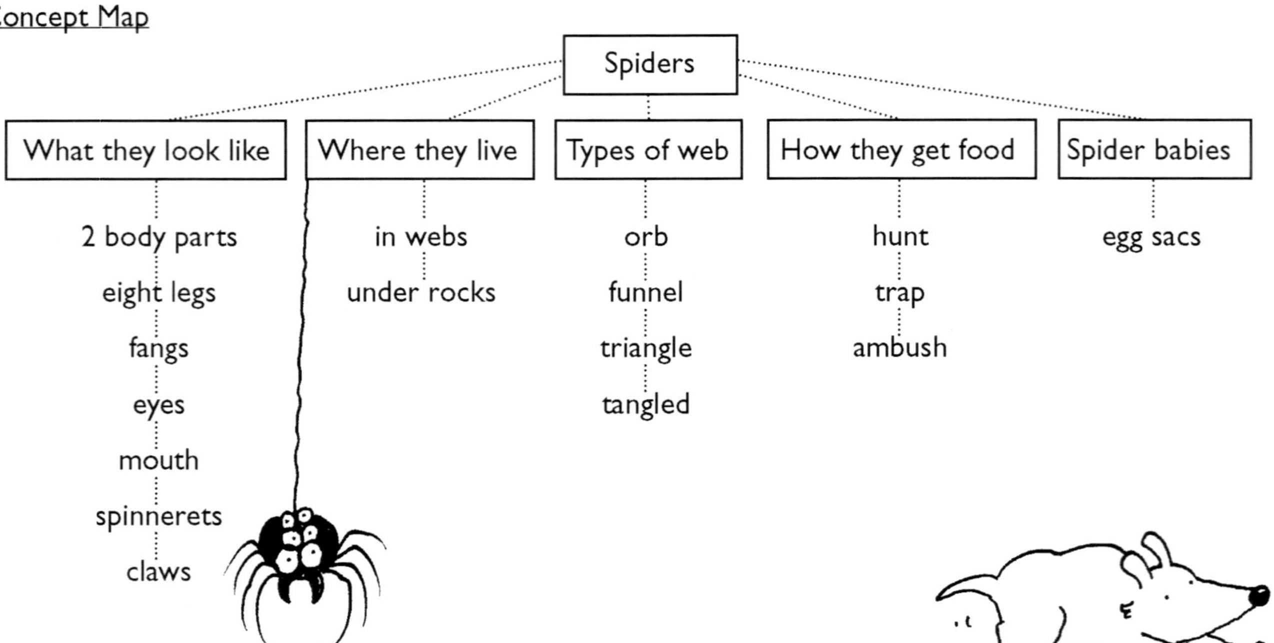

<u>Semantic Web</u>

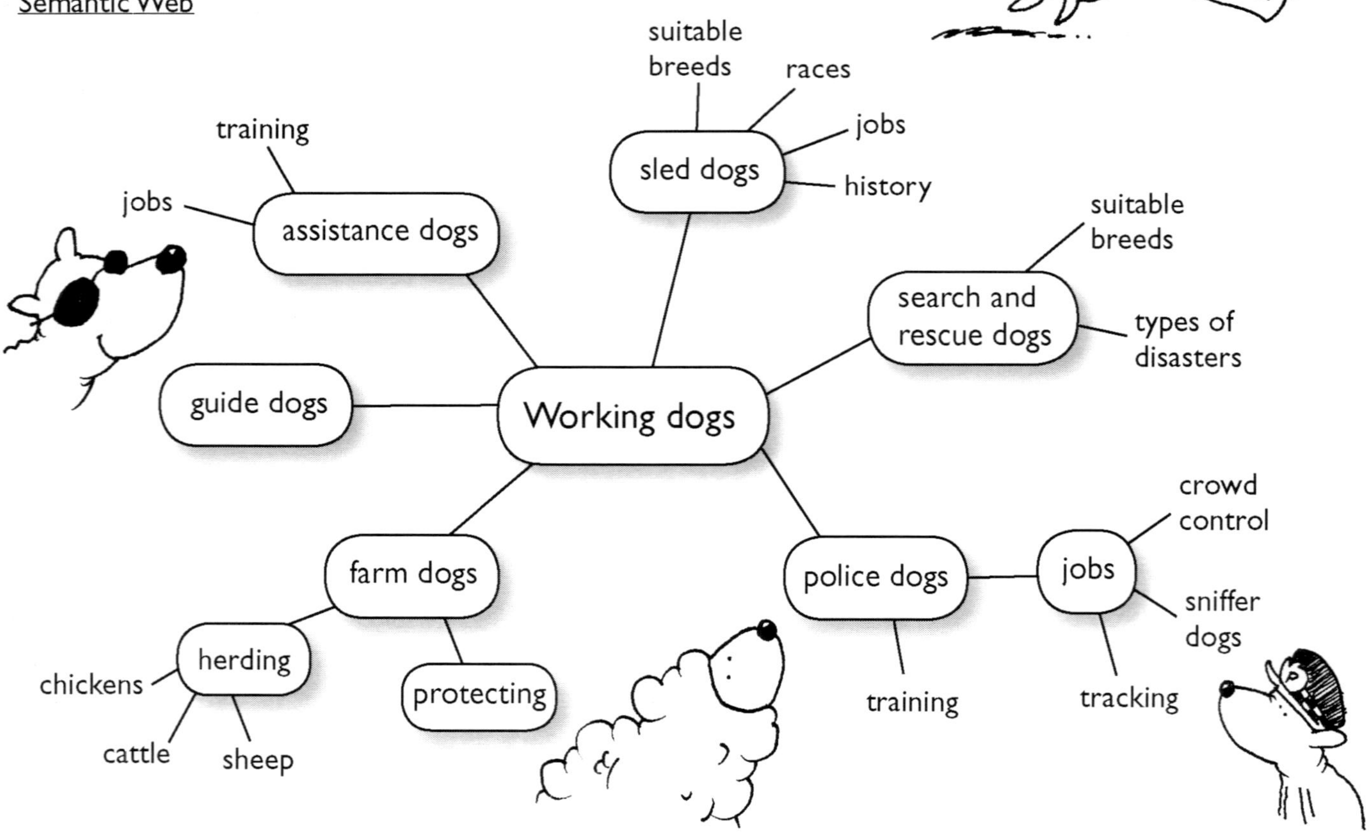

When introducing a new topic to the class, brainstorm a list of questions that students have about the topic, such as *What else would we like to know? Where does it live? How does it look after its babies?* and use these questions to construct a concept map or semantic web.

Dramatisation

Students can dramatise any narrative, poem, concept or situation. Dramatising narratives focuses students' attention on the structure of narratives. In the early stages, student dramatisation often includes a lot of talking but little understanding of the need for complication and resolution. The functions of orientation, complication and resolution can be made explicit during preparation of student dramas or after presentation or performance.

Dramatising a narrative helps students to focus on the relationships between the characters and how this is demonstrated through language choices. The relationship between language users in a situation can be referred to as tenor. The tenor of a situation determines the way language is used. Dramatisation offers great opportunities for students to explore tenor as they take on roles as different characters in different situations. An example would be a group of six-year-olds play-acting a family scene in a supermarket where the student playing 'the child' yells and dominates the parents. Most students in the audience would look to the teacher for confirmation that this behaviour is acceptable in a drama. The value of the drama is that it shocks, and challenges the accepted roles of parents and children. This creates an opportunity to discuss with students the way relationships in a situation determine which language choices are appropriate. (**Dramatisation** allows for planning and preparation for performance, whereas **Improvisation** – see page 17 – does not).

Editing and Proofreading

Editing is when students read over their work to ensure that it communicates what they mean. When students edit their work they look at aspects such as the structure and grammar of the text and their choice of vocabulary to convey the meaning they are attempting to make.

When students are proofreading they are ensuring that their writing is ready for publication. Students need to understand that clear written communication requires correct spelling, punctuation and grammar.

Scan a piece of writing that has some grammatical and/or spelling errors (such as a passage you have written yourself with deliberate errors, or a sample of a volunteer student's work) and display it on an IWB to show students how to proofread a passage. The activity on **Reproducible 4** requires students to check and correct verb forms, and is a useful tool for students to practise their proofreading skills.

Epilogue

An epilogue asks students to predict what happens beyond the end of a narrative. Students need an understanding of characterisation, time frames and issues in the narrative to create an epilogue.

Have students write an epilogue for a class novel or work in groups to create a performance that shows what could happen after the end of a novel. Compare and discuss the validity of each epilogue presented. Students could also create prologues. A prologue would include events that took place before the start of the story, underpinning character behaviour and events in the story.

Freeze Frames

Freeze frames are a series of depictions or frozen moments in time in which a number of scenes are presented in sequence. Students create a scene, freeze to show the audience and then move into position for the next scene and freeze. The audience needs to close their eyes during the transitions between scenes so that the images they see are frozen depictions.

Freeze frames are a good way to revise time connectives, as students need to establish time frames and sequences when creating each scene of their freeze frame. For example, a freeze frame sequence based on a family portrait might go like this:

First the photographer arrived. Then the family got ready. Then the photographer set up the camera. After the family photos were taken, the photographer joined in for a group shot.

Use the template on **Reproducible 5** to create freeze frame cards. Write each scene for the sequence on the card and distribute the cards to groups of students.

Games

1. **Verb/Adverb Improvisation** Photocopy **Reproducible 6** and cut out the cards. Place the verbs in a container. Place the adverbs that tell how in a different container. Have students play in teams. Have each team pick a word from each container and create an **improvisation** to illustrate both words together. Students themselves could create some more word cards.
2. **Alphabet Challenge** Have students play in pairs and give each pair a copy of **Reproducible 7**. Randomly select a letter of the alphabet and tell students to write a word starting with this letter in each column, and shout 'Stop!' when they are finished. As soon as a team shouts 'Stop!', have all students stop and compare their answers. Every correct unique answer scores two points. If another team has the same answer, score one point only for that answer. The team who finished first gets a bonus point if all their answers are appropriate.
3. **What's Your Answer?** Create a deck of cards with a grammar term written on each card. For example: *a saying verb, a doing verb, a proper noun in your school, a proper noun for a place in Australia, a describing adjective for a tree, a describing adjective for a person, a noun group, a sentence* and so on. Place the deck face-down on a table. Have students play in groups. Students take turns to turn over a card. If they answer correctly they win the card. If they answer incorrectly the card goes to the bottom of the deck. The student with the most cards when the deck is finished is the winner.
4. **Quiz** Have students create quiz sheets for their classmates. For example, a proper noun quiz has all proper noun answers. Questions could include: *What is our teacher's name? What is the name of our town? What is the principal's name? What would be a good name for a goldfish?*

5. **Findaword** Ask students to create grammar findawords for each other to solve. The findawords can focus on adjectives, common nouns, proper nouns, verbs or words that tell how (adverbs). A doing verb findaword is included on **Reproducible 8** to get students started.
6. **Label that Picture** Create a set of picture or photo cards from travel brochures, magazines, newspapers and so on. Create a set of grammar cards labelled *noun, noun group, verb, sentence, adjective* and so on. Place cards in two piles face-down on a table. Have students take turns to turn over one of each card and give ten answers. For example, if they turn over a *noun* card, have them name ten nouns in the picture; if they turn over a card labelled *sentence*, have them describe the picture in ten full sentences.
7. **Concentration** Have students play a game of Concentration by pairing a label card with a picture card. For example, one matching pair would be a card labelled *verb: eat* and a card showing a picture of a person eating. Use **Reproducible 9**, or create your own cards. Shuffle the cards and place them in rows face-down on a table. Have students take turns to turn over pairs of cards. If the cards are a match, they keep the pair and have another turn. If the cards are not a match, they turn them face-down again. The student who has collected the most pairs at the end of the game is the winner.
8. **Noun Group Challenge** Write common nouns on pieces of paper and place in a container. Have students play individually or in pairs. Select a noun from the container and call it out. Tell students to write the longest noun group they can for the main noun that you called out. Noun groups can include adjectives, phrases and clauses. If students are not yet familiar with the term 'noun group', tell them to use as many words as they can to describe the noun. For example: *'desk' – teacher's desk, old wooden teacher's desk, old wooden messy teacher's desk, old wooden messy teacher's desk with the cracked surface, old wooden messy teacher's desk that is about to fall apart.*
9. **Memory Out Loud** Have students sit in a circle and take turns to list nouns taken on a picnic, seen at the zoo, bought at a shop, visible in the classroom, found in the home and so on. Each student needs to remember the items already listed and then add their own.

I went to the zoo and I saw a bear.

I went to the zoo and I saw a bear and a zebra.

I went to the zoo and I saw a bear, a zebra and a hippo, and so on.

The game could also be played using verbs.

I went to the park to play.

I went to the park to play and run.

I went to the park to play, run and sing . . .

10. **Suggest a Word** Create a deck of cards with grammar labels such as *noun, verb, adjective*. Add further terms such as *proper noun, common noun, how word (adverb)* as these are introduced to students. Students play by placing the deck face-down on a table. They then take turns to turn over a card and name a word for the label. If the word is correct according to the rest of the team or the adjudicator then they keep their card. Initially you might allow students a free turn when they answer correctly but as students become better at the game and better at grammar terminology you might need to revise the rules and not allow the free turns. The student with the most grammar cards at the end of the game is the winner.
11. **Categories** Have a large number of examples of words for grammar categories such as common nouns *(cat, dog, chair)*, doing verbs *(run, skip, hopped)*, saying verbs *(say, ask, yelled)*, proper nouns *(Australia, Kevin, Bondi)*, adjectives *(soft, sad, cheeky)* and so on written on pieces of paper. Have students work in groups to place the words in their correct grammar categories. Students could compete in teams.
12. **Word Sorts** Use word cards that have been used for various purposes in the room. Have students work in groups to sort the words by a criteria of their choice, such as past tense verbs, saying verbs, synonyms, number adjectives, number of syllables; any criteria is acceptable as long as students can justify their choice.
13. **Snap** Create a deck of playing cards with a grammar label and sample word on each card (such as *noun: cat* or *proper noun: Australia*). Make sure that you have two or four cards for each word. Two or four students can play this game. Shuffle the deck and then deal each student an equal number of cards until all the cards have been dealt. Students take turns placing a card face-up on the table. When a pair is shown the first player to spot the pair calls 'Snap!' and snaps their hand on the pile. The aim is to collect all the cards. When the deck is finished and all the cards have been collected the person with the most cards is the winner.

Hot Seat

In Hot Seat, one student takes on the role of a character in a novel or a famous person in a historical recount, newspaper article, biography or autobiography. The rest of the class acts as interviewers or journalists and asks the student in the 'hot seat' questions about their thoughts, feelings and responses to events in their life. Hot Seat allows students to explore interview techniques and the structure of open-ended questions, point of view, modality and characterisation. Some answers will be based on evidence available to students in the text they have taken the character from. Some answers may not be readily evident but the person in the Hot Seat role should be able to extrapolate how their character would respond. The student in the Hot Seat will need to use thinking and feeling verbs to represent their point of view.

Improvisation

Improvisation involves students acting out a scene without rehearsal or script. It allows students to explore roles and relationships and use language for different purposes. Divide the class into groups then have groups improvise a scene that you suggest, such as 'You are three friends talking about a teacher who you think was unfair about something. Use thinking and feeling verbs to talk about your feelings.' Choose scenes that students can relate to so that improvised conversations are relatively easy for them, at this stage of their schooling.

Mime

Have students write verbs *(eating, jumping, singing, hopped, flew)* and prepositional phrases that tell <u>where</u> *(on a picnic, on the moon, in the shower, under an elephant)* on pieces of paper and place them in separate containers. Students can take turns to select a word or word group from one container (or both containers if they need an extra challenge), and mime the word. The rest of the class needs to guess the answer. These grammar words could also be used for improvisation or as stimulus for narrative writing.

Multi-voice Recitation

In Multi-voice Recitation, students use their voices individually, in pairs, small groups or large groups to recite poems. Individual words in the poem, or lines and stanzas, can be allocated to particular students. Some students can chant echoes or background noises such as onomatopoeic words. Individual voices can recite softly, groups can recite loudly and so on. Sections of the poem can be recited as a 'round'. Have students work in groups to determine how they will present their poem, or organise a whole-class recitation for performance.

Poetry

Different forms of poetry are useful for focusing on different aspects of grammar. For example, Dylan Thomas Portraits are useful for teaching description because they make use of noun groups and adjectives. They commence with a question, then the answer is provided in seven or eight words, usually presented as four pairs of words.

Have you ever seen an emu?

Long-necked, two-legged, beady-eyed, fast runner

Ezra Pound Couplets can also focus on description, as well as the figurative language of metaphor, by saying that one thing is the same as the next in the couplet.

A dolphin speeding through the waves

A shadow too fast to catch

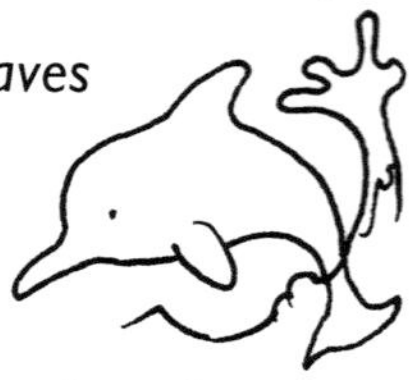

Polarised Debates

This is a less formal form of debate than the traditional type of debate (the parliamentary debate). It is a physical discussion and it supports all students to have a say, rather than discussion being dominated by the few very confident students in a class.

A topic statement is presented and then students who agree with the statement stand on one side of the room. Students who disagree stand on the opposite side of the room. Students who are undecided stand across the middle of the room to make a horseshoe shape. Students learn that it is acceptable to change their opinions as they listen to the convincing opinions of others. Students should move across the room as they change their minds. Usually the polarised debate finishes when every student has had an opportunity to speak at least once.

Jointly construct a written discussion text after the debate. Outline the main points raised for different sides of the issue and then end with a position statement. Model the use of connectives (joining words) such as *on the one hand, on the other hand, alternatively.*

Readers' Theatre

Readers' Theatre is useful to teach students about speech marks, quoted speech, saying verbs and narrators. Choose a section of dialogue in a novel. Then allocate which character's dialogue each student will read. It might be useful to use a narrator to read the rest of the text that is not quoted speech. Readers' Theatre can be useful to demonstrate the voice of the narrator. In a first person narrative a character's alter ego could read the part of the narrator. If the author is the narrator, discuss third person narrative.

Retelling

Have students retell a story or recount. They need to listen and then they need to sequence their retelling using time words (such as prepositions and adverbs) and joining words (connectives). In retelling, they will use the thinking skills of remembering and understanding; however, if they can retell events from the point of view of different characters (such as the three little pigs or the big bad wolf), they will be using the higher-order thinking skill of applying.

Role-play

Have students role-play interactions in various situations between various people. Role-playing provides students with opportunities to use spoken language in different contexts with different audiences and purposes. They can role-play classroom or school-based situations, pretend to be at the shopping centre requesting help from shopkeepers, making purchases, on the telephone with ambulance officers in an emergency, requesting and giving directions, offering assistance, interviewing for television and so on.

Students can also take on the roles of story characters and build on their roles in different situations where they interact with others.

Role-play allows for exploration of the use of vocatives (distant, formal, polite, friendly). Students can also explore the use of body language and facial expression in varying situations and how use of these non-verbal cues is affected by the relationships between the language users (tenor).

Students can explore roles and relationships using puppets.

Storyboard

A storyboard is a shooting script for a film or video. It is like a cartoon version of a story, with the story divided into frames. Have students work in groups to create a storyboard, deciding whether the frames show close-ups, mid shots or long shots, based on what is significant in that part of the story.

Students can create storyboards for poems, play scripts and narratives. The storyboard will show the noun groups (people, places, animals and things) that are important in the text. Students can be asked to focus on particular aspects of grammar to label the frames in their storyboards, such as verbs, noun groups, quoted speech and phrases that tell where. This example shows a three-panel storyboard of a poem, using verbs as labels.

Frogs squat fatly

waiting for the rain

they can smell the clouds.

Story Map

Have students draw a map based on a story read together in class. Story maps allow students to visually represent the setting for a narrative. Students need to consider, in particular, prepositional phrases that tell where, describing adjectives, noun groups, and connectives that show time or cause (joining words).

Sculptures

Have students create a sculpture using their bodies to depict a noun. Students in lower primary will tend to find it easier to represent concrete nouns. However, students operating at more advanced stages (or students who are bodily-kinaesthetic learners) might be able to creatively express abstract nouns such as *love, hate, peace, quiet, happiness*. Fluid sculptures add movement to the sculptures. Usually the movement is repetitive.

Have fun with grammar!

- use it and play around with it
- make fun of it
- distort and exaggerate it
- play games with it
- enjoy it as a subject worthy of your students' time

There is no need for grammar to be onerous, so take care with your own attitude.

Remember: Grammar is fun!

Annotated Models for Different Types of Texts

The following pages include text models taken from the *Grammar Rules!* student books. The models are annotated to show aspects of grammar relevant in the various types of texts. Not all types of texts will necessarily be relevant to your students.

Imaginative – Narrative

Social purpose

- To entertain, enlighten and/or to teach a lesson or moral

Forms

- Picture books, novellas, novels, storytelling, puppet shows, play scripts, ballads, storyboards

Visual elements

- Photos, drawings, illustrations in print media
- Gestures, facial expression and body language in film and other oral presentations

Structure

- Orientation: the scene is set for events; characters and settings are introduced
- Complication: a problem is introduced for characters to deal with
- Events in the plot occur
- Resolution: characters resolve problems (either solve them or deal with them in some other way) and grow from the experience
- Comment or coda

Wednesday and Ruby

Once upon a time there was a puppy called Wednesday. She had a basket to sleep in, her own bowl to drink from and toys to play with. Best of all she had her very own human family.

One day there was a huge storm. The wind howled. The rain thundered. The trees swished and swooshed. The branches smashed and crashed. Wednesday was scared. She ran away.

By the time the storm was over Wednesday didn't know which direction was home. She walked and walked. Finally, she came to a sheep in its paddock. The sheep's name was Ruby.

"I'll help you find your family," said Ruby.

Extract from *Grammar Rules! Student Book 1*, page 54

- time words and phrases
- 3rd person personal pronoun
- proper noun
- noun group with adjectives
- onomatopoeia
- past tense doing verb
- thinking verb
- where phrase
- quoted speech
- saying verb

Social purpose

- To describe people, places, animals or things

Forms

- Narrative poetry, conversations, scientific reports, information reports

Structure

- Orientation: introduction to the topic
- Logical sequence of descriptions about aspects of the topic
- Conclusion: a summing-up statement
- Judgement or evaluation (optional)

A Moreton Bay Fig Tree

Extract from *Grammar Rules! Student Book 1*, page 30

Social purpose

- To explore different points of view on a topic

Forms

- Newspapers and magazines, journals, talkback radio, panel discussions, polarised debates, conversations

Structure

- Orientation: introduction to the issue
- Opinion for one side of the issue supported by reasons
- Differing opinion supported by reasons
- Summing up
- Recommendation or judgement (optional)

word chain of nouns and pronouns (reference chain)

being verbs

When I Grow Up

Some people in my class want to be pop stars and movie stars when they grow up. They want to be rich and famous.

Other people in my class want to be police officers or firefighters. They want to help people and have adventures.

I want to be a teacher when I grow up. I want to be the boss and I like helping little children.

Extract from *Grammar Rules! Student Book 1*, page 46

connective to compare and contrast

evaluative language

connective to add

thinking and feeling verbs

Informative – Explanation

Social purpose

- To tell how or why things work or how or why things are the way they are

Forms

- Science journals, textbooks, reference material

Visual elements

- Flow charts, cycle diagrams and other types of diagrams and illustrations

Structure

- General statement about the topic (could include a how or why question)
- Sequence of information – usually in cause and effect sequence or time order
- Concluding statement (optional)

common nouns

HOW SEA ANIMALS BREATHE

Whales are mammals. They breathe air just like humans. Humans and whales need the oxygen in the air. Whales have one or two nostrils on top of their heads. These nostrils are called blowholes. The whale comes to the surface and blows out all its used air. Used air is air with no oxygen left in it. Then the whale breathes in fresh air. Now it can dive again.

Fish breathe oxygen too. Their oxygen is dissolved in the water. Fish have sets of flat gills on both sides of their mouths. A fish sucks water into its mouth then pushes the water back out through its gills. As the water flows past the gills, the gills pick up all the oxygen. This is how fish breathe under water.

present tense

technical terminology

connective to show time

noun group

connective to show cause

Extract from *Grammar Rules! Student Book 2*, page 72

doing verbs

Persuasive – Exposition

Social purpose

- To present a strong point of view on a topic

Forms

- Speeches, letters to the editor, editorials, talkback radio, parliamentary and polarised debates, television current affairs interviews

Structure

- Position statement
- Arguments presented in logical order with supporting reasons
- Restatement of position/summing up
- Recommendation (optional)

thinking verbs

being verb

adjective

connective to add

3rd person personal pronoun

emotive word

high modality to reinforce a viewpoint

1st person personal pronoun

The Best Pet

I think that mice are the best pets anyone can have. They are extremely cute. They are entertaining and fun to watch, especially if you give them an exercise wheel and other toys. Also, they are really small. They don't take up a lot of space in a house or apartment. They are simple to care for—just keep their home clean. They don't cost very much to buy and they are cheap to feed. These are the reasons why I believe that mice make the best pets.

Extract from *Grammar Rules! Student Book 2*, page 20

Persuasive – Advertisement

Social purpose

- To persuade people to buy a product or to take a course of action

Forms

- Leaflets, catalogues, brochures, posters, magazines, radio, television, cinema, newspapers, billboards

Visual elements

- Visual elements are significant in all advertising except radio. Visual elements include slogans and icons, colour, font, design, layout, photographs, images of famous people and places.

Structure

- Opening question/s or statement to capture attention
- Sequence of claims about the product with arguments to support the claims
- Restatement of position: call to action

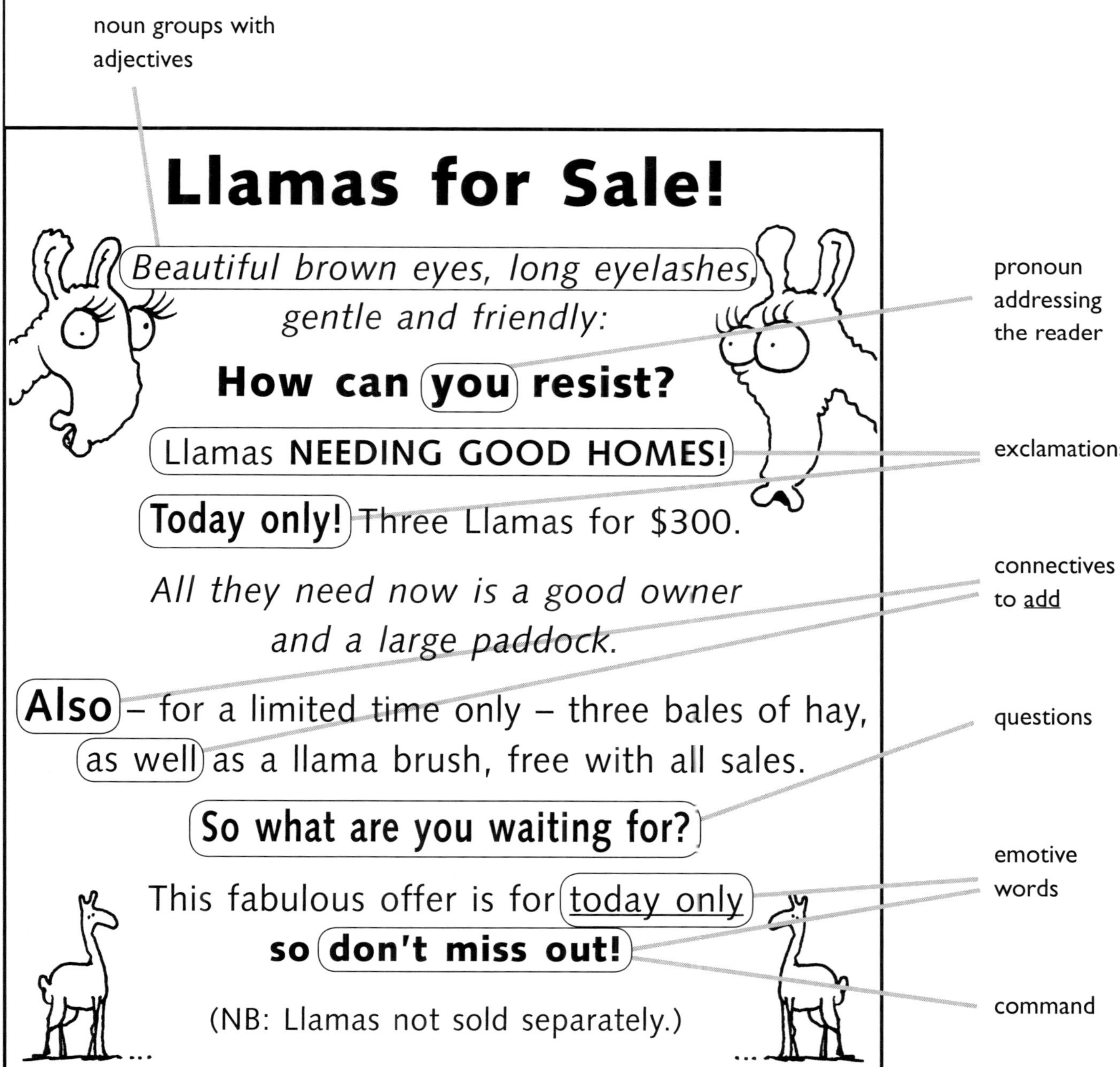

Extract from *Grammar Rules! Student Book 2*, page 50

Informative – Information Report

Social purpose

- To provide information about a general class of thing

Forms

- Articles, reference material, journals, internet, encyclopedias

Visual elements

- Diagrams, graphs, photographs, charts, illustrations

Structure

- General opening statement: introduction to the topic
- Information about aspects of the topic, in a logical sequence
- Paragraphs based on topic sentences
- Reorientation or finishing-off statement (optional)

common noun

present tense

3rd person personal pronoun

KOALAS

Koalas are marsupials. They live in large community groups. Koalas have thick, grey, woolly fur. They live in trees. They are excellent climbers. Koalas are mostly active at night. They sleep for 18 to 20 hours every day. Koalas only eat eucalyptus leaves. Koalas make interesting noises. Male koalas grunt and bellow. Female koalas bellow too. Female koalas make special noises for their babies. They murmur, hum and make clicking sounds. When a koala is frightened its scream sounds like a human baby's scream.

where phrase

noun group with adjectives

doing verb

technical terminology

word chain of nouns and pronouns (reference chain)

being verb

Extract from *Grammar Rules! Student Book 1*, page 72

Social purpose
- To tell someone how to do something

Forms
- Recipes, cookbooks, directions, instructions, rules, cooking shows, gardening shows, manuals, conversations, 'how to' demonstrations

Visual elements
- Photographs and diagrams

Structure
- Statement of goal or purpose
- List of ingredients and/or equipment
- Method or steps in logical sequence as commands
- Caution/warnings (optional)

Magic Potion

This potion turns baby brothers and sisters into playful puppies.

common nouns

Ingredients:

- Two ground up snail shells
- Three puppy hairs (any breed)
- One dollop of goblin snot
- One nail clipping from the baby

noun group with number, describing and classifying adjectives

Method:

1. Mix all ingredients in a large bowl.
2. Place one spoonful of the mixture on the baby's hairbrush.
3. Chant three times, "Playful, peaceful puppy!"
4. Be patient! The potion can take up to five minutes to work.

command with doing verbs in theme position

where phrase

present tense

steps in numbered order

Warning: This potion only lasts for one hour. To make it stick for more than one hour, add some glue at Step 1.

time phrase

Extract from *Grammar Rules! Student Book 1*, page 62

Informative – Recount

Social purpose

- To retell a series of events

Forms

- Letters, emails, diaries, biography, autobiography, newspaper articles, conversations, television news and current affairs programs

Structure

- Orientation
- Series of events in chronological order
- Summing up or reorientation
- Personal comment or judgement (optional)

time word

proper nouns

past tense doing verb

1st person personal pronoun

word chain of nouns and pronouns (reference chain)

connective to show <u>cause</u>

noun group with adjective

connective to show <u>time</u>

saying verb

Dear Gran and Pa,

Yesterday we went to the pet shop. I asked Mum for a puppy but she said that dogs make Dad sneeze. So we decided that goldfish were the best pets for us. First we had to buy a fish tank and gravel. Then we chose a bridge for the fish to swim under and some plants. Finally I got to choose two fish. I picked a black one and a gold one. Their names are Midnight and Sundance. Dad says we'll phone you next Sunday.

Love from Sara

Extract from *Grammar Rules! Student Book 2*, page 22

Social purpose

- To respond to something, such as an event, an artwork, an issue or an aspect of nature

Forms

- Book, film and art reviews; excursion reviews; diaries and journals; conversations; poetry

Structure

- Introduction or orientation to establish the context
- Exploration of different aspects of the topic: an outline of events, descriptions, thoughts, feelings
- Conc usion: judgement, opinion or recommendation

noun group

evaluative language

GIANT PANDAS

My lucky grandpa went on a fabulous trip to China last month. He came back with photos of his visit with giant pandas in Chengdu. I really love his panda photos. The pandas look so soft and cuddly. They are huge. Grandpa said he had to wash his hands and wear a surgical gown and gloves, like a doctor, so that he didn't give the pandas germs. He fed carrots to one panda and held it in his lap while it ate. I would really love to go to Chengdu one day to see the pandas.

3rd person personal pronoun

thinking and feeling verb

1st person personal pronoun

doing verb

figurative language – simile

emotive language

Extract from *Grammar Rules! Student Book 2*, page 42

Assessing Grammar

The purpose of assessment is to find out what students know and understand, and to use this information to plan further learning opportunities. Assessment strategies include gathering evidence in a wide variety of ways and making judgements about teaching and learning, based on the evidence.

Formative assessment processes assist teachers to monitor ongoing teaching and learning. Formative assessment makes use of teacher–student interactions, observation of students as they are involved in tasks, analysis of work samples, peer assessment, and student self-assessment and reflection.

Summative assessment processes include analysis of work samples and other evidence of student learning, with a view to using these to inform further planning for teaching and learning.

Samples of students' written texts can be photocopied, analysed and stored in student portfolios to monitor progress and determine areas of need. Anecdotal records can be made about students' spoken texts, or spoken presentations can be filmed or recorded.

Revision units are included in the *Grammar Rules!* student books at units 6, 12, 18, 24, 30 and 35. These can be used as revision or for testing purposes. Each Revision unit deals with aspects of grammar covered in previous units. Student performance on these units will show whether further revision is required.

During **writing conferences**, discuss the purpose of the writing and the appropriate type of text and text form to achieve the social purpose. Discuss the structure of the text, the cohesion of the text as a whole (for example, use of connectives, word chains), use of paragraphs and visual elements, and grammar at the sentence or clause level, and the level of word groups, phrases, words and word parts.

Finding time to conference with every student about every piece of writing is a challenge for teachers. Parent helpers can be of some assistance as long as they are trained in what to look for, what to suggest and how to assist students.

Peer conferences can also be useful as long as students are provided with specific criteria to focus on in each other's work. Students can be taught to firstly examine text structure and content to see if it matches purpose and audience. Next they should examine whether the text is effective grammatically. Then they can consider the finer details of punctuation and spelling.

Student self-assessment supports student autonomy and self-management. Encourage students to reflect on their own learning, effort and achievements. Students can use personal journals to record evaluations of their strengths and needs, as well as their responses to classroom activities.

Each *Grammar Rules!* student book includes a pull-out section with a Student Writing Log. The pull-out section can remain in the student book for safekeeping or it can be easily removed and stored in students' writing folders. The Writing Log provides a way for students to keep track of the types of texts and text forms they are writing, and the grammar they are attempting to use in the context of their writing. The log includes a column where students rate their own writing, as well as a 'Where to next?' column for them to write their aims. Teachers can also include their comments and suggestions. The Writing Logs are a useful tool to refer to in conference with your students. They also support students' independence and encourage students to develop responsibility for their own writing tasks and grammar learning.

Work Samples

Collect samples of students' written work for analysis of achievement and progress.

Samples of students' written texts are included on the following pages. They have been annotated to demonstrate for teachers how to assess students' grammar in written texts.

Analysis of Student Work Samples

The following pages include annotated samples of students' written texts.

Narrative Work Sample

Context

The class had explored fairytales and folktales. Students had discussed the structure of a narrative text. They were reminded about the functions of the orientation, complication, series of events and resolution in narratives and were asked to write a fairytale of their own.

consistent use of past tense verbs

appropriate noun/ pronoun word chain (reference chain)

proper noun for a name

some use of describing adjectives

time phrase

connective to show <u>cause</u>

Uense abon a time there livd a littal girl she livd with one brother and one sister allso a Step Mather the littal girls name was Emily she was vere brite she had to werck evry day she didn't get enerest one day a letter came it sede that all of uor famle can came to a boll so they went to the boll and thea left Emily behind she began to cry but sadanle an Angl cam for the rof the Angl said you are going to the boll the Angle said get me a banana so Emily got an banana and the Angle tond the banana into a bote and get me a cat she said ...

Work sample from 6-year-old student (typed by teacher with student's spelling)

Assessment Comments

Structure

The student shows creativity and an understanding of narrative structure. The text begins with an orientation to set the scene and introduce the main characters. The complication in Emily's life arises when the family goes to the ball without her. The series of events in the plot commences when an angel appears and begins to fix things for Emily.

Language Features

There is consistent use of 3rd person personal pronouns, and appropriate noun/pronoun reference chains. Proper nouns are used appropriately.

There is some use of describing adjectives.

The use of 'suddenly' adds drama and tension to the plot.

The student needs support to understand the concept of a sentence, and in using punctuation marks, quoted speech and paragraphing.

The student needs to use thinking and feeling verbs to represent Emily's feelings so that the reader can understand the character's motives and feelings.

The student needs to learn about a range of saying verbs to avoid overuse of *said*, which is used four times in the narrative.

Description Work Sample

CONTEXT

Students were asked to write a description of an animal that they are personally familiar with, such as a pet.

proper noun needs a capital letter

being verb

noun group with adjectives

1st person personal pronoun

where phrase

no apostrophe for possession

figurative language

doing verb

3rd person personal pronoun

Patches

My dog patches is very big. He is white and has big brown patches all over him that is why we called him patches. Patches is very fluffy and always wags his tail. His eyes are big and black. On the tip of patches tail it is brown and it looks like it has been dipped in chocolate. Patches is always very playful and happy he likes to chase balls and play with the other dogs in the park when we take him.

Work sample from 8-year-old student (typed by teacher with student's spelling)

ASSESSMENT COMMENTS

Structure

The student's description is comprehensive. The use of a simile, *looks like it has been dipped in chocolate*, engages the reader.

The description includes a very basic orientation, *My dog patches*, and proceeds straight to the description.

The description provides a detailed picture of aspects of the topic – the dog's size, colouring, fur and behaviour.

A conclusion, judgement or final statement giving the writer's opinion about the dog might improve the structure of the text and give the text a form of completion.

Language Features

Noun groups with adjectives give a detailed description of aspects of the topic.

The 1st and 3rd person personal pronouns are used accurately.

The dog's size could be more accurately portrayed, perhaps using simile *(as big as . . .)*.

The description could have used a classifying adjective to describe the breed of the dog.

The student must be careful to capitalise all proper nouns, and include apostrophes for possession.

Discussion Work Sample

Context

The school had recently held a cake day to raise money for a charity. Families had donated cakes to be sold to students at morning tea time.

The class was divided into groups to discuss the topic: 'The school should hold a cake day every Friday'. At first students could only think of arguments that supported or agreed with the statement because they had enjoyed the special treat of cakes and sweets. Their discussion broadened when they were challenged to consider the points of view of others. When they had finished talking they were asked to write their discussion using the scaffold as follows:

Discussion Scaffold

We discussed the topic …

Some people think …

Other people think …

We think …

One group jointly constructed the following text.

> We discussed the topic if the school should have a 'cake day' every Friday.
>
> Some people think it's a good idea. It gives money to children who don't have enough food. They don't have water. The cake day was fun.
>
> Other people think that it's not very good for children to eat cakes when those children are starving. Also some children can't bring a cake to school. Also cakes make you fat.
>
> We think it would be better to just ask for money to send to the people.
>
> Work sample from a group of 7- to 8-year-old students (typed by teacher with spelling corrected)

arguments not linked

confusing reference chain

only connective

2nd person personal pronoun

Assessment Comments

Structure

The discussion adequately presents the different points of view. The students have used the Discussion Scaffold effectively, including an orientation, arguments for one point of view with supporting reasons, arguments for an opposing point of view with supporting reasons, and a concluding statement with a judgement and a recommendation.

However, the arguments are not presented logically or introduced coherently. For example, *The cake day was fun* follows the sentence *They don't have water.* There is no logical connection between the two simple sentences.

Language Features

Students understood and could explain each argument in their text because they were involved in the discussion; but the meaning is not clear to a reader. Students need to learn that a reader needs reasons for opinions to be clearly written because a reader will not know what is in the writer's head.

The word chains for reference are confusing. For example, *children* is used to refer to children at the school as well as children in other countries.

The mix of 1st, 2nd and 3rd person is also confusing.

Also is the only connective used. It is a connective that adds one thing to another, the simplest kind of connective.

Explanation Work Sample

Context

Students planted seeds in three containers of cotton wool. They kept one container in a cupboard in the dark. The other two containers were kept on a windowsill exposed to sunlight but only one received water. Students watched as the seeds that were watered and kept in sunlight grew. Class discussion focused on what was happening with all the seeds. Students kept a growth diary for the three seed containers. Technical terms such as *root* and *shoot* were written on class charts. The text below was dictated by a student to a parent helper who typed it on the computer. The student was asked to explain how seeds grow.

past tense

connectives to show sequence

How seeds grow

First we plant the seed. Then we put the seed in the sunlight. Then we water the seed every day. After a few days the seeds grew roots to help them drink the water. Then the seeds grow a green shoot. The green leaves grew straight up like grass. I didn't eat them.

Work sample from a 7-year-old student (typed by helper with spelling corrected)

mix of singular and plural

present tense

technical terminology

simile

personal comment

Assessment Comments

Structure

This attempt at an explanation is written as a recount of events. The student shows understanding that explanations present a sequence of phenomena. However, the text is more a recount than an explanation. It uses time connectives and past tense verbs. An explanation would also be written in a sequence but explanations make use of present tense verbs and connectives to link through cause and effect as well as time. For example, *The seed sends out a root so it can drink the water.*

Language Features

Connectives are used effectively to show time sequence; however, the student swaps between past and present tense.

The student uses accurate technical terminology – *sunlight, root, shoot.*

There is a mix of single and plural nouns to refer to the same thing *(the seed/seeds).*

Use of simile is usually inappropriate in an explanation.

The personal comment at the end is relevant in a recount but inappropriate in a scientific explanation.

Exposition Work Sample

Context

Students talked about pets and then wrote their personal opinions about which pet is best.

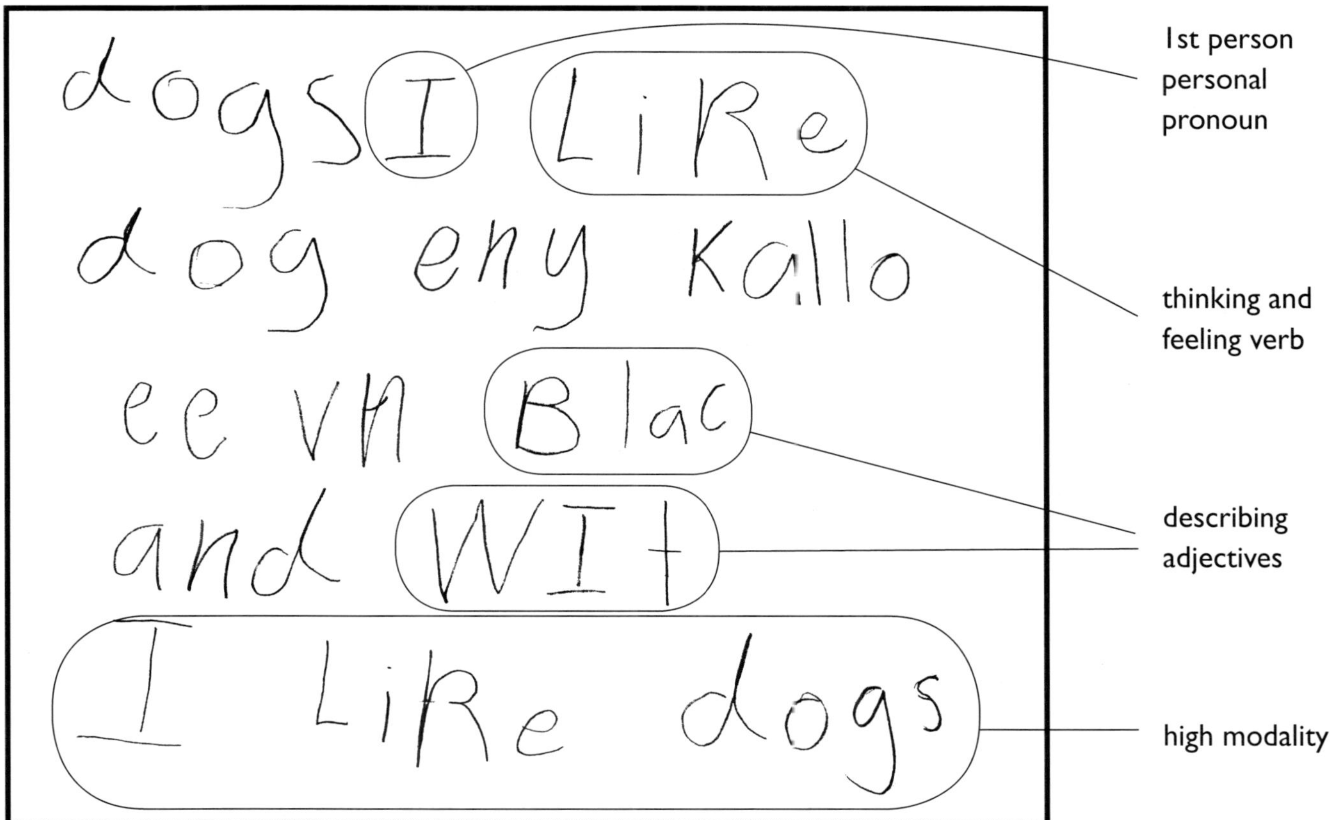

Work sample from a 5-year-old student

Assessment Comments

Structure

The student shows understanding of the structure of exposition texts and the need to present a point of view. The text begins with a position statement and ends with a restatement.

The student has expressed a point of view but not given reasons. For example, they could have written *I like dogs because they are friendly*.

Language Features

The student uses 1st person personal pronouns appropriately.

Thinking and feeling verbs are used to express a point of view.

The text uses high modality, which is appropriate for an exposition.

The student needs to learn to support opinions with reasons, connecting the reasons with words such as *because*.

The student spells phonetically (*wit* for *white*; *eny* for *any*) and uses some familiar high-frequency words (*like*). The student uses lower and upper case letters interchangeably. There's no evidence of punctuation.

Advertisement Work Sample

Context

Students examined advertising leaflets and then wrote an advertisement of their own to sell products of their choice to classmates.

inaccurate homophone

describing adjectives

high modality

emotive language

appropriate noun/ pronoun word chain (reference chain)

accurate homophone

no commands with doing verbs in theme position

Would you like to by lemonaid?

Its sweet and very yummy.

It will give you lots of energy.

Icy cold.

Lemonaid for sale!

$2 a glass

Work sample from a 7-year-old student (typed by teacher with student's spelling)

Assessment Comments

Structure

The student has used an opening question to attract attention, followed by a sequence of claims about the product. The opening question was modelled on a number of advertisements examined by the class, which began with questions such as *Would you like a holiday?* All questions seen in the real advertisements elicited a 'yes' answer, whereas the student's question *Would you like to by lemonaid?* might not elicit a 'yes' response.

The advertisement is brief and to the point.

Most advertisements end with a call to action (for example *Buy our lovely lemonade!*), which is lacking here.

Language Features

The student shows understanding of high modality and emotive language in advertising, and uses describing adjectives to promote the product.

There is an appropriate noun/pronoun reference chain for the product.

The student needs to be careful with homophones – *by* is used instead of *buy*.

The advertisement could be strengthened with some commands with action verbs in theme position.

Information Report Work Sample

Context

Students were required to work independently to research an animal of their choice and construct an information report to read to the class. This copy is the student's final presentation.

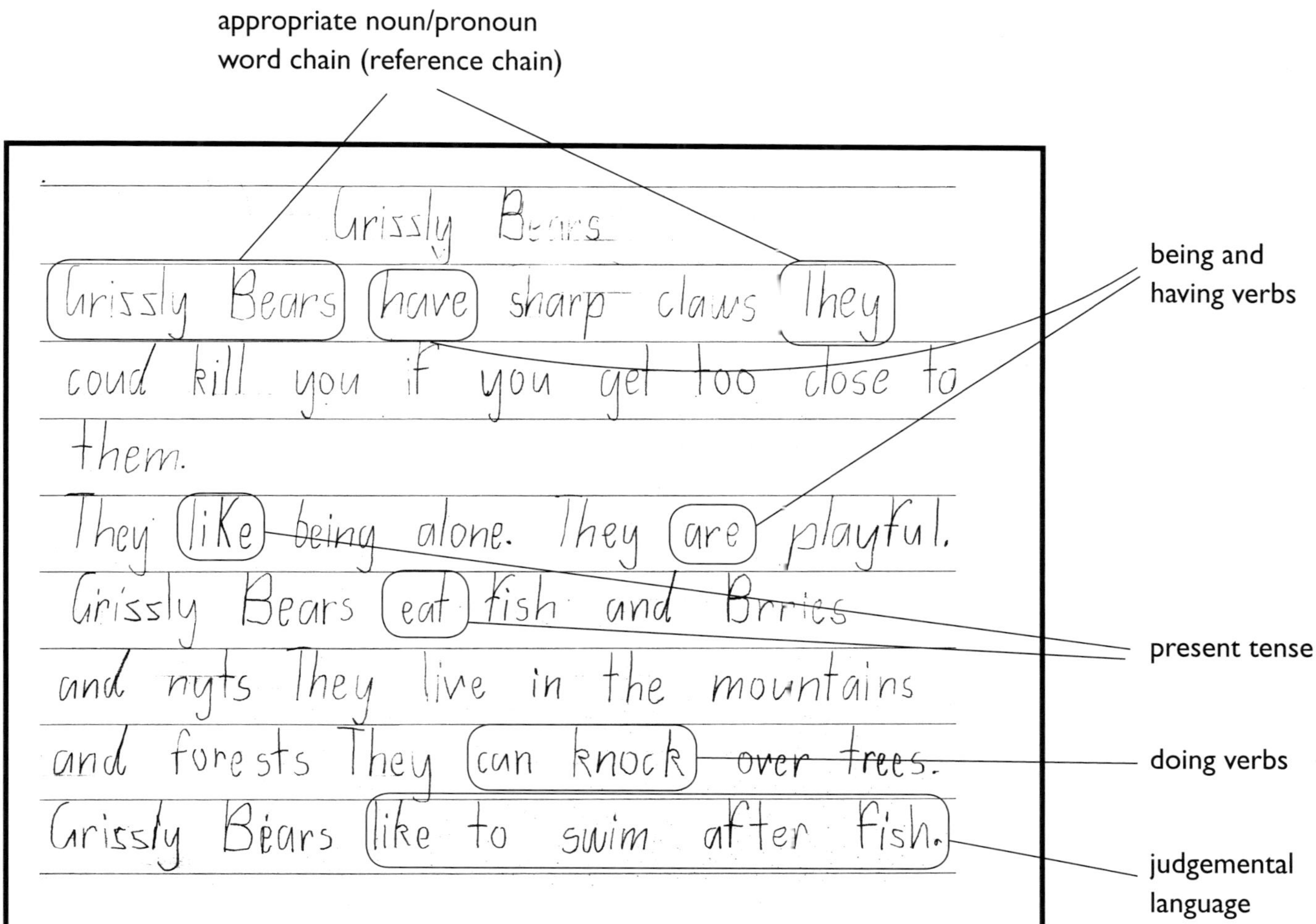
Grissly Bears

Grissly Bears have sharp claws They coud kill you if you get too close to them.
They like being alone. They are playful.
Grissly Bears eat fish and Brries and nyts They live in the mountains and forests They can knock over trees.
Grissly Bears like to swim after fish.

Work sample from a 7-year-old student

Assessment Comments

Structure

The student provides information about aspects of the topic.

There is no general opening statement. The student proceeds straight to the description of bears.

There is no finishing-off or summing-up statement.

Language Features

The student uses being and having and doing verbs appropriately.

The information report includes information about where bears live, what they eat and their behaviour. Most information is not well grouped: *like to swim after fish*, for example, could be grouped with the sentence that finishes *eat fish and berries and nuts.*

The student uses mainly simple sentences with the connective *and*. The student could have used connectives such as so to show cause, for example *Grizzly bears have sharp claws so they . . .*

The student mostly uses present tense appropriately: *have, are, live, like to swim;* except *They could kill you if you get too close.*

A judgement is made in stating that bears *like to swim after fish*. Judgemental language is usually inappropriate in an information report, which needs to contain fact not opinions, so the student should be taught to state only the facts.

The information provided was not fully explained. For example, when the report was read to the class students had further questions they wanted answered about bears: Why do they knock down trees? How do they play? Who or what do they play with?

Procedure/Recipe Work Sample

Context

Students had examined examples of instructions and recipes and were familiar with the structure and grammar. Students then engaged in a cooking activity where they assisted the teacher in making nachos. The list of ingredients was written on the board. After they had eaten, students were asked to write the method for others to follow to be able to cook the nachos. One student's method is included below.

> # Texan Nachos
>
> **Method**
>
> We stired the baked beans and the onions and the mince until it was all cooked then we put in tomato sorse and mixed it around. We ate it with corn chips and cheese.
>
> Work sample from a 6-year-old student (typed by teacher with student's spelling)

1st person personal pronoun

past tense verb

connective to show sequence

personal comment

confusing reference

Assessment Comments

Structure

The student has written a recount of the cooking activity rather than a recipe.

The sequence is chronological but not completely accurate. The mince and onions were cooked before the baked beans were added and heated through.

The personal comment is inappropriate in a recipe: *We ate it . . .*

Language Features

The student has used connectives effectively to show time sequence.

The 1st person personal pronouns are inappropriate in a recipe. Recipes are usually written as commands, with an ellipsis for 'you': *[You] Stir the mixture.*

Past tense verbs are not appropriate in a recipe that requires present tense verbs for the ongoing nature of the actions.

The student has not made use of commands, or doing verbs in theme position.

The 3rd person singular pronoun *it* is firstly used to refer to the plural noun group *the baked beans and the onions and the mince*. The student should either have used *they* or *the mixture*. The pronoun *it* is used a second time to refer to the completed nachos. The student needs help to ensure word chains for reference are consistent and accurate.

The student shows some understanding of capital letters for sentence beginnings and the use of full stops at the ends of sentences. The text has a title.

Recount Work Sample

Context

Students were given a five-page diary booklet, labelled Monday to Friday, and asked to write entries each day for a week.

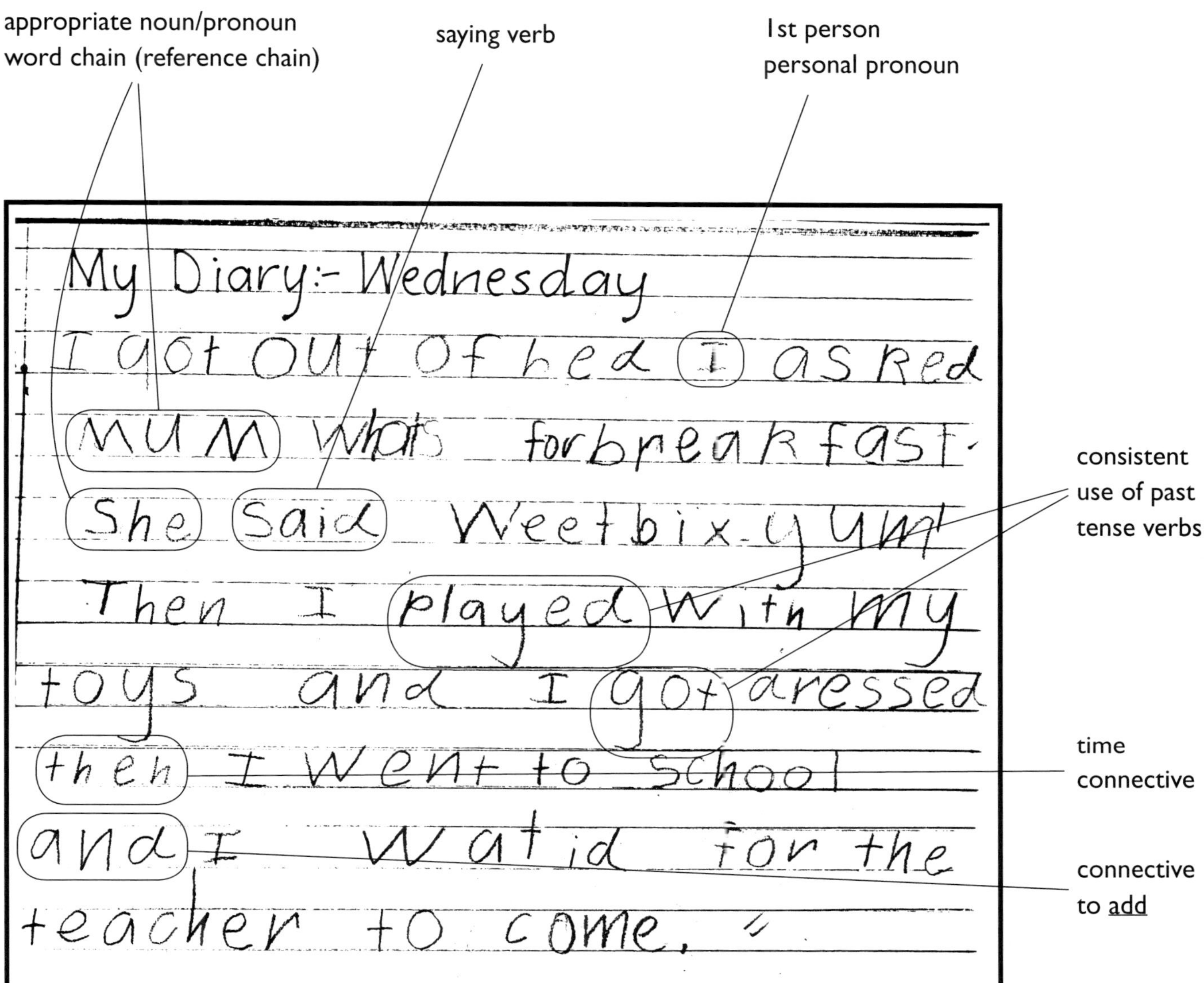

Work sample from a 6-year-old student

Assessment Comments

Structure

While the student has written a series of events in chronological order, they have provided no orientation or summing up/personal statement.

The student provides a sequence of events but gives little insight to any personal thoughts or opinions, except for *yum*.

Language Features

The 1st and 3rd person personal pronouns are used appropriately.

Past tense verbs are used accurately and consistently; however, the student could be taught to use a larger range of time connectives and time phrases such as *This morning, after that, when*.

There are no describing words. The student could be taught to use adjectives to add descriptions.

There is limited use of evaluative words or thinking and feeling verbs to represent the writer's point of view.

Response Work Sample

Context

The teacher read the class a book of short stories and then asked students to write a book review. The teacher listed the title, author and illustrator of the book for the class to copy. Students were reminded to include a brief description of the book's contents in their reviews and to give their opinions about the book.

1st person personal pronoun

being verbs

simple sentences used throughout

evaluative language

overuse of *funny*

1st person personal pronoun

thinking and feeling verb

high modality

Book Review

The teacher read us a book called *The Cat on the Mat is Flat*. The author is Andy Griffiths. The illustrator is Terry Denton. The book is nine funny stories. The words rhyme. The book is easy to read. Everyone in my class enjoyed the stories. They are very funny. The teacher showed us the pictures. The pictures are very funny too I like this book. I like the pictures. I think everyone will like this book. Even adults will like this book.

Work sample from 8-year-old student (typed by teacher with spelling corrected)

Assessment Comments

Structure

The work sample is well-structured, with an orientation to establish context; an exploration of different aspects of the topic (contents, words, illustrations, humour, who would enjoy it); and a concluding statement with a judgement and recommendation.

Language Features

The student uses 1st person personal pronouns *I* and *us* appropriately.

The student uses evaluative language to present opinions: *enjoyed, funny, I like*.

High modality is used appropriately to assert a point of view.

The student uses simple sentences throughout the review with no attempt to link clauses or use connectives.

The statement *The book is easy to read* needs to be qualified to state exactly who might find the book easy to read; for example, *most students in year 2*.

There is limited use of descriptive words: *funny* is repeated three times.

STUDENT BOOK 1

SCOPE AND SEQUENCE

This scope and sequence chart is based on the requirements of the Australian Curriculum.

Unit	Unit name/ Type of text	Clause to whole text level			Word and word group level		
		Sentences and clauses	Cohesion: theme, pronouns, lexical chains, connectives	Mood and modality, language and vocabulary	Nouns and noun groups	Verbs and verb groups	Adverbs and prepositional phrases
1	**Things in the Garden** Information report/ Diagram				common nouns		
2	**A Fish** Information report/ Diagram				common nouns		
3	**Shopping List** Information report/ Shopping list				common nouns		
4	**A Family Tree** Information report/ Diagram				proper nouns		
5	**Our Weather Chart** Information report/ Weather chart				proper nouns; common nouns; describing adjectives		
6	REVISION						
7	**Jobs on the Farm** Information report/Map			commands	nouns		
8	**At the Playground** Recount				nouns	doing verbs	
9	**Class Rules** Information report/Rules			commands; exclamations		doing verbs	
10	**The Fire Brigade** Recount				nouns		adverbs and prepositions to tell when
11	**Goodbye Elvis** Recount				adjectives; proper nouns	saying verbs	adverbs to tell when
12	REVISION						
13	**A Moreton Bay Fig Tree** Description	sentences		commands	nouns; adjectives		
14	**Jokes** Jokes/Questions and answers	sentences		questions			
15	**Our Favourite Pets** Information report/ Graph				singular and plural nouns	doing verbs	
16	**My Fish** Description			synonyms	describing adjectives; nouns	doing verbs	
17	**Fish Tank Diorama** Procedure/Instructions			commands	nouns	doing verbs	
18	REVISION						

Unit	Unit name/ Type of text	Clause to whole text level			Word and word group level		
		Sentences and clauses	Cohesion: theme, pronouns, lexical chains, connectives	Mood and modality, language and vocabulary	Nouns and noun groups	Verbs and verb groups	Adverbs and prepositional phrases
19	**Sleepy Cat** Description/Poem		personal pronouns	rhyme	nouns	doing verbs	
20	**Dear Aunty Selma and Uncle Kenan** Response/Letter				proper nouns for place names; common nouns		
21	**When I Grow Up** Discussion	sentences		questions; question words: *who, what, where, when, how, why*; opinion			
22	**The Lonely Dragon** Narrative		conjunctions (connectives): *and, but, so, because*		proper nouns		
23	**How We Get Our Milk** Explanation/Flow diagram	sentences		fact and opinion; rhyme			
24	REVISION						
25	**Wednesday and Ruby** Narrative			onomato-poeia			adverbs and prepositional phrases to tell when
26	**Buy Now!** Exposition/Advertisement			alliteration; contractions	adjectives; proper nouns		
27	**Sharks** Exposition			antonyms		thinking and feeling verbs	
28	**Cinderfella's Jobs** Procedure/Instructions			commands	nouns	doing verbs	adverbs to tell how
29	**Magic Potion** Procedure/Recipe		logical order		number adjectives		
30	REVISION						
31	**Life Cycle** Explanation/Cycle diagram			compound words	nouns	doing verbs	
32	**How to Get Home** Procedure/Directions					doing verbs	prepositional phrases to tell where
33	**Book Review** Response/Book review	quoted speech; speech marks	conjunctions (connectives): *and, but, so, because*	questions; opinion	describing adjectives		
34	**Koalas** Information report		cohesion: repetition; pronouns		describing adjectives; nouns	saying verbs; doing verbs	
35	REVISION						

Grammar Focus: Nouns
Type of Text: Informative – Information report/Diagram

Student Book 1
Unit 1

The unit focuses on common nouns. Tell students that they can remember that '***nouns name***' because both words start with ***n***.

Label things in the classroom with common noun labels: *desk, wall, door, chair, plant, cupboard* and so on.

Use the nouns in Unit 1 to start some categorised word banks of common nouns (ie magical story nouns: *swan, frog, elf, giant wishing well, castle, ogre;* and garden nouns: *hose, bucket, leaf, plant, tree, bush, dirt, soil, seed)*. Brainstorm some more lists of nouns, for example animal nouns, school nouns and so on. Students can refer to these word banks for their own writing and spelling.

Type the sentences students write for question 5, about real or magical gardens. Create a large garden mural with combinations of magical and realistic nouns, and display with students' sentences.

There are lots of activities and games to play with students to reinforce the concept of the common noun:

Play a game of Snap with matching pairs of common nouns (see page 17 for instructions on Snap). Create the card deck using the same nouns as labelled in the room and the same nouns used in Unit 1 (*flower, tree, bird, ball* and so on) to reinforce the reading and spelling of these words.

Use words from the deck of Snap cards to practise alphabetical order.

Play a game of *I spy* and name nouns in the school (for example, *I spy a noun beginning with t – teacher*).

Play *Simon/Simone says* with nouns. *Simone says touch a chair; touch your toes.*

Trace outlines of students' bodies and then label the noun parts: *head, shoulders, knees, elbows, uniform, shoe, sock, hat.*

Teach students to sing the song *Heads, shoulders, knees and toes.*

Play spelling bingo with the nouns.

Grammar Focus: Nouns
Type of Text: Informative – Information report/Diagram

Student Book 1
Unit 2

Display information books with diagrams and illustrations that include factual labels. Discuss factual texts and the kinds of labels that give information, such as the labels on the fish in Unit 2.

Compile a class book of animal diagrams with labels. Have students work in pairs and have each pair choose an animal. Ensure that students choose animals with varied body parts such as insects, birds, sea mammals and amphibians. From the factual books on display in the room, ask students to draw an animal and attach labels to name the animal and its body parts with nouns.

Have each student write a sentence about a pet they own or would like to own. Create a class display of sentences, or a class book of pets or posters of pets. Have students use pictures from magazines, draw the pets or use photographs of their own pets.

Investigate the RSPCA website in your state for information about pets and the availability of posters to display in the classroom. A local vet might be available to talk to students about pets.

When students undertake the **Try it yourself!** activity, specify that they draw 'incredible' pets such as dragons or elephants rather than 'realistic' pets. Transcribe their sentences or have parent helpers type them for a display with pictures and illustrations.

Share picture books and other stories about pets.

Write rhyming word pairs for some of the nouns from Unit 2. Make decks of Snap cards or Concentration game cards for students to match the rhyming nouns, for example *eyes/pies, gills/frills, tail/snail, fins/pins* (see pages 16 and 17 for instructions on Concentration and Snap). Ask parent helpers to make the cards or challenge students who are capable in this area to write noun pairs.

Grammar Focus: Nouns
Type of Text: Informative – Information report/Shopping list

Student Book 1
Unit 3

Read the words on the shopping list and discuss the way the words are organised into categories. Create a list of places to buy groceries and other items – markets, fruit and vegetable shops, butcher, baker, supermarket, chemist, pet supplies stores, newsagencies, book stores, health food stores, hair salons and so on. Brainstorm a Concept Map that lists nouns for items available to purchase at each place (see page 14 for instructions on Concept Maps).

Examine letterbox leaflets for grocery items.

Have students create their own dinner collages. Have each student glue magazine pictures onto a paper plate, glue the plate to cardboard and label the dinner with nouns. You can encourage healthy foods and link Unit 3 to health. Discuss healthy foods and the categories of foods that should be eaten every day. Or, you might like to let students create the most unhealthy dinner they can think of, to have fun with their food nouns.

Create graphs of students' favourite fruit, favourite party food, favourite canteen item and so on.

Make a 'healthy breakfast' chart. Include noun labels and collage pictures for milk, fruit, cereal, toast, eggs, fruit juice, water, yoghurt, rice, bread, fish, noodles and so on.

Make a 'healthy lunch' poster using photos of students in the class eating healthy lunches. Label the photo poster with nouns. Make a slideshow on a school computer or use the healthy lunch photos in a screensaver program.

Grammar Focus: Proper nouns
Type of Text: Informative – Information report/Diagram

Student Book 1
Unit 4

Talk to students about nouns that are 'common' or everyday, and nouns that are called 'proper' because they are the important names of people or particular places. Tell students that all proper nouns start with a capital letter. Exaggerate the word 'proper' so that students learn to associate it with names for people, places, days and months.

Discuss the differing family structures of students in the class – single parent, step families, guardians and so on. Ensure all students' family circumstances are respected by others in the class. Have students create family trees. Invite parents to share information about their family history. Discuss with students the proper nouns they use for parents (for example, *Mum, Mother, Mama*) and grandparents (for example, *Grandpa, Pop, Nonno*) and any cultural differences in these titles that are applicable in your classroom. Display students' family trees in the classroom with proper noun labels and photos if they are available.

Undertake a 'crazy portrait' collage activity. Label containers with the following common nouns: eyes, nose, mouth, eyebrows, ears. Cut art paper into strips. Give students the strips of paper and have them draw two eyes on one piece then place it in the labelled jar. Then have them draw a nose, a mouth, and so on on other strips of the art paper and place the face parts in the correct jars. Then give students art paper with an oval-shaped head outline already copied onto it. Tell students to give their head some hair using paint, crayons, crepe paper, coloured paper, fabric scraps or wool. Then have students collect random facial features from the jars and glue them onto their head outlines. Tell students to give the portraits proper noun names such as 'Green-Eyed Gomez' and then display them in the room. Ensure that students do not make fun of each other when naming their crazy portraits.

Grammar Focus: Proper nouns, adjectives
Type of Text: Informative – Information report/Weather chart

Student Book 1
Unit 5

Create a class list of words for days of the week and months of the year. Point out to students that these words are proper nouns. Teach the students to recite the days of the week in sequence. Teach students to chant the rhyme '30 Days Has September'. Turn the rhyme into a rap chant with body percussion and 'beat box' sound effects.

Display a monthly calendar in the classroom with significant events such as students' birthdays and excursions. Display a weekly timetable that lists routines such as library and assembly.

Point out that the months of the year are associated with particular seasons and weather patterns: spring, summer, autumn, winter; wet, dry, storm season.

Have students work in groups to create posters for the seasons. Write the months of the year as proper nouns on the posters and have students collage or draw pictures of clothing or activities that match the season. If you live in an area that does not experience a cold winter you can point out on a map the areas where it snows and show students pictures of clothing and activities that are appropriate, and read picture books that deal with seasons or seasonal events.

Ask students to brainstorm adjectives that can describe 'day' and 'night', for example:

hot, windy, cold, cloudy, stormy, rainy, bright, humid, sunny *<u>day</u>*

cold, dark, windy, black, scary, spooky, hot, sticky, noisy *<u>night</u>*

Provide students with paint and art paper and have them paint abstract pictures of a day or a night using the describing words in the lists. For example, they could paint a windy night or a stormy day. Tell them to label their paintings with adjectives.

Grammar Focus: Commands
Type of Text: Informative – Information report/Map

Student Book 1
Unit 7

The child in the text *Jobs on the Farm* has a list of jobs to do. The child needs to follow the instructions provided with the map. Point out to students that the instructions are numbered so that the child will follow them in the correct sequence. Point out that the instructions are written as commands. When someone gives you orders or tells you what to do, these instructions are called commands.

Ask students to suggest commands or orders that family members give them at home, or orders that they receive at school (for example 'Line up. Walk into the room. Unpack your bags.'). Compile a chart.

Have students work in pairs to pretend they are in the army. Tell them to order each other around taking turns for one member of each pair to be the sergeant and the other to follow orders. Give examples of commands: 'March to the fence. Stop there. Turn around. March on the spot. Jump on the spot.'

Endeavour to make students aware of the doing word at the start of each command that actually tells what has to be done.

Draw and label a large farm mural. Have students cut out and paint paper sheep, chickens, cows and pigs to glue onto the mural. Read farm story books to students. Brainstorm a list of farm animals. Label farm animals on the mural of a farm. Talk to students about the nouns for things that can be produced on a farm: *wheat, corn, wool, eggs, beef, milk, vegetables, fruit, honey*. Talk about plant and animal produce and also discuss processing, which enables people to use products such as flour. Create some flow diagrams that show students processing sequences, if this is relevant to your class.

Grammar Focus: Doing verbs
Type of Text: Informative – Recount

Student Book 1
Unit 8

Tell students words that represent an action are called doing verbs or action verbs. Brainstorm a class list of doing verbs for actions in the school. Give the list a title such as *What we do at school*, and list things like *read, draw, play, listen, run, pretend, act, count, sing* and so on. (It does not matter, at this stage, if students list saying verbs or thinking and feeling verbs with the doing verbs. They will learn the distinctions as they progress through the units.)

Question 5 asks students to write the doing verbs a hand can do. Have students trace around their hands or provide them with photocopied hand outlines. Tell them to decorate their paper with drawings and to write on the hand all the things their hands can do using doing verbs. Display their hands.

Integrate this unit with a unit of work on the senses. Use noun and verb labels: eyes can see; ears can hear; tongues can taste; brains can think; noses can smell; skin can touch.

Create a touchy-feely bag with items inside students need to feel and give noun labels (sandpaper, modelling clay, cotton wool, comb, plastic dinosaur, teaspoon, laundry peg, bulldog clip . . .).

Blindfold students in turns and have them touch textured objects like cold cooked soggy spaghetti, kiwi fruit, rambutan, coconut shell. Have students use describing words (adjectives) to describe the way things feel: smooth, spiky, prickly, slimy, soggy, cold. Create a list of words that describe. (Be aware of any allergies students have, and make sure they don't taste any of the food items.)

Grammar Focus: Commands, exclamations
Type of Text: Informative – Information report/Rules

Student Book 1
Unit 9

Brainstorm a list of class rules for your classroom. Where possible try to write students' suggestions in a positive way. For example, 'Don't run in the classroom' could be written 'Walk indoors'. Compare your list of class rules with the *Class Rules* in the student book.

Discuss rules for other situations, such as road rules, beach safety, swimming pool safety, use of medicine and use of chemicals such as household cleaning products. Ask students why rules are needed. Talk about the purpose of rules: to keep people safe. Talk about the consequences of not following rules. For example, some students like to balance their chairs on two legs. A class rule might be 'Keep all four chair legs on the floor'. A consequence of disobeying the rule might be to tip over and bang your head on the floor. Another class rule might be 'Never walk around with scissors in your hand'. Discuss the potential consequences of disobeying this rule.

Tell students about commands that are also exclamations because they are said in surprise or anger. Ask what exclamation they might make if they see someone carrying scissors and about to step on something slippery: 'Stop! Be careful!'

Point out the doing verbs at the start of most commands. Even commands that start with a negative such as 'Do not walk' still start with a verb or verb group.

Talk about the way a person's voice and facial expression can make a command seem really bossy. Have students work in pairs. Have one member of each pair be a parent and the other a child. Tell parents to be really bossy and command their child: 'Tidy your room'. Swap roles. Have parents give commands in a less bossy manner. Discuss the differences made by voice, facial expression and body language.

Grammar Focus: Time words
Type of Text: Informative – Recount

Student Book 1
Unit 10

Read students picture books that have an obvious time sequence such as days of the week, seasons, or times during a day. Ask your school's teacher/librarian to suggest titles to you such as *The Very Hungry Caterpillar* by Eric Carle (Picture Puffin Books). Point out to students the words and word groups that help to sequence events. Numbers also help to sequence events. Numbers are used to sequence instructions so that you know what to do first and what to do next. Numbers are used to tell a sequence in sport and games: first, second, third.

Jointly construct a recount with the class. Recount an event that has happened in the school recently. Or, take the students for a walk around the playground and stop at various points to look at or listen for something specific. Write a recount of your walk when you return to the classroom. Point out the words that help to sequence the events in time: *then, next, after* and so on.

Talk to students about people in the community who help them: doctors, nurses, dentists, teachers, vets, police. Use gender-inclusive language to label these people and ensure that students recognise that each occupation can be done by males and females.

If possible, organise a visit to your school by the fire brigade and/or members of the police force. Jointly construct a recount after the visit. Make sure students recognise that the recount retells events that have happened in the appropriate time sequence.

Grammar Focus: Saying verbs
Type of Text: Informative – Recount

Student Book 1
Unit 11

Point out that *Goodbye Elvis* is a recount. Ask students to tell you why it is a recount – it retells events that have happened and is written in a time sequence.

Read students picture books where characters speak or have dialogue. Point out the words that tell that the characters are speaking, such as *said, yelled, asked, announced, whispered*. If you have Big Books then display the writing so that students can see the saying verbs.

Have students work in pairs. Tell students to say hello to each other. Tell students to repeat their greetings but this time to whisper. Then have them shout, giggle, hiss, snort, snicker, meow, bark, grunt, wail, whine and cackle the greeting. Write the saying verbs on chart paper as you call them out for students. Add to the list whenever you find new saying verbs in stories you are reading to the class.

Write some sentences on the board or on chart paper and include saying verbs and speech marks. For example, *"Hello, Toby," giggled Farid.* Ask students for suggestions about sentences to write for each of the saying verbs listed on the chart paper.

Make a class book that makes use of animal saying verbs. Write a sentence suggested by students on each page, for example *"Hello," neighed the horse. "Would you like some milk?" mooed the cow.* Have each student illustrate a page. Highlight the saying verbs.

Grammar Focus: Sentences
Type of Text: Informative – Description

Student Book 1
Unit 13

A Moreton Bay Fig Tree is a description of a particular tree. Talk to students about the structure of the text. It describes the parts of the tree (its trunk, branches and roots) and then tells about the tree's age. It also tells how the birds, insects and children benefit from the tree for shade and homes. It ends with a summing-up statement. *A Moreton Bay Fig Tree* also gives the writer's personal opinion about the tree. Ask students what that opinion is. Point out the full stops and capital letters in the text. The text consists of nine sentences. Reinforce the idea of a sentence. Ask nine students to read a sentence each in turn.

Photocopy **Reproducible 3** (page 77). Cut the text into separate sentences and have students work in pairs to complete a jigsaw cloze activity (see page 13 for instructions on jigsaw cloze). A few different arrangements will still make sense, although the orientation and conclusion must remain the way they are written.

Have students read out variations on the sequence that still make sense and are appropriate in a description. Then cut each sentence into individual words or word groups and have students create sentences for a sentence cloze activity (see page 14 for instructions on sentence cloze).

Conduct sentence cloze with sentences written by students for each other. Have students write sentences (check their punctuation and grammar to confirm that they have actually written proper sentences). Tell them to cut their sentence into separate words. Place each sentence in an envelope or container of its own. Include some commands in the sentences so that students learn to use a verb in theme position. A challenge for gifted students is to mix two separate typed sentences in the one envelope and have students organise the two from the jumble.

Grammar Focus: Questions
Type of Text: Imaginative – Jokes/Questions and answers

Student Book 1
Unit 14

Tell students that questions are sentences that ask something. Questions end with question marks rather than full stops. Read picture books that include questions such as *Where is the Green Sheep?* by Mem Fox and Judy Horacek (Penguin). Use these texts as models and have students create pages of their own for a class book. For example, based on *Where is the Green Sheep?* students could use the same pattern of statements and questions and write a story book filled with fairytale creatures: 'Here is Red Riding Hood and here is the wild wolf. But where is the hairy fairy?' Or, they could create a book with animals. For example, 'Here is the wide elephant and here is the narrow snake. But where is the cheeky chimp?' If you use *Where is the Green Sheep?* take the opportunity to discuss antonyms, and make a class list of 'opposites'.

Display joke and riddle books in the classroom and encourage students to examine the questions involved in these.

Have students work in groups of three or four. Provide each group with a large sheet of chart paper and a crayon or felt-tip pen. Glue a magazine picture to the centre of each sheet. Pictures could be of anything: scenery, families, individual people, houses and so on. Have students write questions based on the picture on their sheet. Display and discuss students' questions.

Grammar Focus: Singular and plural nouns
Type of Text: Informative – Information report/Graph

Student Book 1
Unit 15

Create a chart with two columns headed *Single* and *Plural*. In the *Single* column, write singular nouns from students' spelling texts or nouns for pets or things in the classroom. Use *one* or *a* or *an* in front of each noun: *a child, one cake, an elephant*. In the *Plural* column, write the plural form of each noun, with a number adjective: *two children, three cakes, many elephants* and so on.

Point out to students the ways to spell plural words by adding an –s or an –es to the end of the word, or by changing letters inside the word: *foot → feet; man → men; woman → women.* Also make a list of words that do not change their spelling: *fish, sheep.*

Share counting books with the class. These books begin with a single noun and then continue with plural nouns to label numbers of things. Create a class picture book of single and plural nouns and have students illustrate their own pages.

You could specify a book about pets or animals. Or, you could allow students to create their own nouns for their page on any topic they choose.

Survey students and then create graphs for other topics such as favourite fruit, TV show, game, sport, outdoor activity and so on. Then have students work in small groups to write reports that use single and plural nouns to explain the graphs.

Have students work in pairs according to the pet they nominated for the **Try it yourself!** graph. Tell pairs to jointly construct instructions for looking after their chosen pet. Remind them that instructions are commands and need to have doing verbs to start them off.

Grammar Focus: Adjectives, synonyms
Type of Text: Informative – Description

Student Book 1
Unit 16

Remind students that adjectives are words that describe. Adjectives can tell colour, shape, size, texture and appearance. They can describe factually or they can give an opinion.

Fact: *the <u>green</u> snake*

Opinion: *the <u>lovely</u> snake*

Show students an object, or a photo or picture. Ask them to suggest adjectives that describe. Discuss the difference between adjectives that tell a fact and adjectives that tell an opinion.

Use a Big Book to demonstrate the function of adjectives to describe. Cover the adjectives in the Big Books with sticky notes. Read the story to students and ask them to suggest alternative adjectives using the illustrations and the story context to influence their suggestions. The adjectives suggested might be the adjectives in the text or they might be synonyms for the actual adjectives used in the story.

Write students' suggestions on the sticky notes. Re-read the story and discuss the effect of the different adjectives on the story. The following narratives are available in Big Book format and include adjectives suitable to use in this cloze activity.

We're Going on a Bear Hunt by Michael Rosen, illustrated by Helen Oxenbury (Walker Books)

Owl Babies by Martin Waddell, illustrated by Patrick Benson (Walker Books)

Have students work in small groups to jointly construct descriptions of places, people, animals or things.

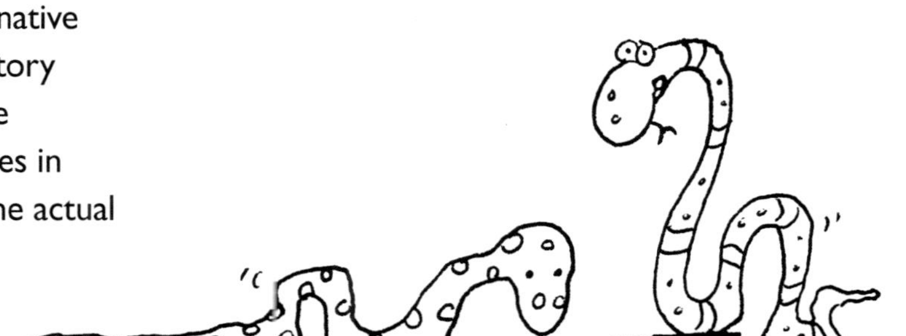

Grammar Focus: Doing verbs in commands
Type of Text: Informative – Procedure/Instructions

Student Book 1
Unit 17

Discuss the function and structure of instructions with students. Point out the goal in the heading, the list of equipment needed and the method as a series of steps written in logical or number order. Display instructions for other activities such as board games, origami or using equipment. Point out to students that often instructions will include visual elements such as photographs and diagrams. Display non-fiction book samples of instruction texts in the classroom.

Students have been introduced to commands in earlier units. Ask students what they notice about the wording in the 'What to do' list. They should notice that the doing verb is at the start of each sentence.

Present students with some oral sentences and have them state as a group or individually whether each one is a question, a statement or a command. You might also revise exclamations, if appropriate for your class.

For example:

I lost my pencil.

Have you seen my pencil?

Get a new pencil.

My pencil was on my desk.

Pick that up, please.

It's broken!

Examine Big Book stories with students and discuss the punctuation marks used for sentences, commands and exclamations (ie full stops, question marks and exclamation marks) and their function in the texts.

Grammar Focus: Pronouns, rhyme
Type of Text: Imaginative – Description/Poem

Student Book 1
Unit 19

Have students perform the poem *Sleepy Cat* as a Multi-voice Recitation (see page 18 for instructions on Multi-voice Recitation).

Divide the class into groups. Allocate a scene from the poem *Sleepy Cat* to each group and have each group paint a poster to illustrate their scene: getting Cleopatra from the pound, Cleopatra sleeping on Daddy's lap, sleeping on brick walls in the sun, sleeping on Mummy's chair, sleeping in all sorts of places. Display the posters and label them with a phrase that tells where, for example: *Cleopatra sleeps <u>on the car</u>; Cleopatra sleeps <u>in the bathtub</u>; Cleopatra sleeps <u>under the rosebush</u>; Cleopatra sleeps <u>on the dog</u>.* Alternatively, create a class book.

Point out to students that when you talk or write about the cat you say *Cleopatra, she* or *her*. *(We got her at the pound.)* Point out that *she* and *her* are pronouns that are used for Cleopatra instead of repeating the cat's name all the time. Read the poem to students repeating *Cleopatra* to replace the pronouns *her* and *she*. Point out to students that repeating *Cleopatra* makes the poem sound clumsy and repetitive.

Point out to students that different pronouns are used for boys and girls (males and females) and things that are not male or female.

the girl → she/her *the boy → he/him*
the door → it

Point out that plural pronouns have no gender.

the girls → they *the boys → they*
the chairs → they

Make sure students understand that a pound is an animal shelter.

Use a Big Book narrative to conduct a cloze activity using sticky notes to cover the pronouns.

You might like to point out that *everywhere* is a compound word – it's made up of two individual words, *every* and *where*.

Explore the use of rhyme in the poem *Sleepy Cat*. Read picture books that make use of rhyme.

Grammar Focus: Proper nouns for places
Type of Text: Persuasive – Response/Letter

Student Book 1
Unit 20

Read the letter to students. Ask them what the letter is about. The letter gives Lana's response to a visit to the aquarium with her aunt and uncle. It begins with an orientation and then describes the animals Lana saw.

Display books of sea creatures so that students can find pictures of the animals Lana saw at the aquarium. Particularly show students illustrations or photographs of the spiralled, corkscrew eggs of the Port Jackson shark.

Create a sea-creature display. For example, have students make sea jellies: cut paper plates in half for the sea-jelly bodies. Use a hole punch to make holes along the straight edge. Tie long strips of crepe paper to the holes for the sea jelly's tentacles. (Note: Sea jellies are not fish so should not be called jellyfish.)

The largest sea jellies can measure two metres across the bell and have up to 30 trailing tentacles. Sea jellies are eaten by turtles. Turtles sometimes eat floating plastic bags that look like sea jellies and the turtles die. Display this factual information with the sea-creature display. Ask students to write their responses to information about sea creatures, to add to the display.

Revise common and proper nouns. Names for places are nouns. If it is an everyday place it is a common noun: *beach, country, road*. If it is a particular place it is a proper noun: *Manly Beach, Christchurch, Sydney Road*. The same rule applies to names for people and pets.

Teach students how to write addresses on envelopes before they complete question 6 in their student books:

- No punctuation marks are used in addressing envelopes.
- Shortened forms are used for proper nouns: *St, Rd, Mr, Ms*.
- Addresses are written in this order: name, street, city or suburb, state, postcode, country.

Grammar Focus: Questions
Type of Text: Persuasive – Discussion

Student Book 1
Unit 21

When I Grow Up is a discussion text. Students learn to express an opinion and support their opinions with reasons. Read the sample text and discuss the opinions presented and the reasons given.

Remind students that sentences start with capital letters and end with full stops, question marks or sometimes exclamation marks. Read each sentence in *When I Grow Up* pausing at each full stop. Point out that each sentence makes sense on its own. It is a complete message or thought. The word groups presented at question 2 are not all complete thoughts: only three make sense *(I will buy a sandwich. Follow the path. Laura has a new watch.)*. Two are statements and one is a command. Ask students to identify the command with its doing verb at the start *(Follow the path.)*.

Who, what, where, when, how and *why* are words that are good question starters. Read picture books to students and then ask them *who, what, where, when, how, why* questions about the narratives.

Have students brainstorm questions that they want answers for when introducing a new topic for study. For example: 'What would we like to know about humpback whales?', 'Where do they live?', 'What do they eat?' and so on.

Demonstrate the writing of a discussion text. Collate students' answers for question 6 about their favourite book and television show. Begin the discussion text with an orientation, for example *Many children in our class enjoy watching television because …* Write students' opinions and the reasons they have for choosing a favourite. End the discussion with a restatement of the topic and then state your own opinion and reason.

Grammar Focus: Joining words
Type of Text: Imaginative – Narrative

Student Book 1
Unit 22

Read *The Lonely Dragon* to students. Have students read it back to you, one sentence at a time, pausing after each full stop. Ask students:

Why did the dragon live alone?

Why did the dragon decide to leave its mountain home?

What did the dragon search for in the far corners of the world?

What doing verb did the knight do? *(killed)*

What doing verbs did the dragon do? *(fly, search)*

Have students underline the common nouns in the text (for example, *dragon, land, parents, knight, friend, home, world*).

Talk to students about the purpose of words like *and, so, but,* and *because* in texts. Tell students that these words join parts of sentences or join ideas in sentences.

Have them use a joining word to finish oral sentences such as:

We put rubbish in the bin ...

We tidy the classroom ...

We use quiet voices ...

We listen to the teacher ...

We like to run inside ...

We like singing ...

Ask students to suggest alternative endings for each sentence using as many of the joining words as possible.

Read picture books about dragons. Draw and paint one large class dragon. Use picture book dragons as models. Or, you might have students draw and paint their own dragons. Have students write or suggest describing adjectives for dragons to display with the paintings *(scaly, green, spiky, fierce, ferocious, lonely, sad, friendly)*. These paintings and adjectives could be displayed with students' narratives for the **Try it yourself!** activity.

Grammar Focus: Fact and opinion
Type of Text: Informative – Explanation/Flow diagram

Student Book 1
Unit 23

Point out to students that the text *How We Get Our Milk* is an explanation. It explains the process involved in getting milk from the cow to the shops for people to buy. Point out to students that explanations are often accompanied by visual elements such as flow diagrams, cycle diagrams, photos and illustrations. Display any explanation texts, books and posters available in your school for students to examine.

Point out the structure of the explanation. It consists of a series of steps in logical order or chronological order (time order). Talk to students about the sequence and what it would mean if the sequence got out of order. Explanations are good texts to use for jigsaw cloze to assist students to understand the importance of logical order (see page 13 for instructions on jigsaw cloze).

Talk to students about milk. How much milk do students drink each day? Why is calcium important for healthy bones? and so on. Make sure students realise that cows have milk to feed their babies, because cows are mammals. Talk about other animals that feed their babies milk, such as humans, whales, dogs, horses, kangaroos, elephants and so forth.

Talk to students about the difference between facts and opinions. Create a chart that has two columns labelled *Fact* and *Opinion*. Write a milk fact in the *Fact* column, such as *Mammals feed their babies milk*. Write an opinion in the *Opinion* column, such as *I love chocolate milk*. Have students write a fact and an opinion onto strips of paper and attach the paper to the correct columns on the chart. Encourage students to write about milk but allow them to write any fact or opinion they choose. Also allow them to use the factual books on display in the classroom to find facts.

Grammar Focus: Onomatopoeia, time words
Type of Text: Imaginative – Narrative

Student Book 1
Unit 25

Tell students that stories or narratives are about characters. They can be human or animal characters. Display and share a range of narrative books with the class. Ask students to identify the characters in the story *Wednesday and Ruby*. Ask them to retell what happened to the characters, what problems the characters faced and how the characters overcame their problems.

Talk about the structure of narrative texts. Narratives need an orientation to introduce the characters and the setting. Then something needs to happen to the characters. These are the events in the story. Narratives need an ending where the characters overcome their problems.

Remind students of the function of time words in texts. Time words help to sequence events and tell the reader or listener the order of events. Time words are especially useful in narratives and recounts. Time words include days of the week and months as well as words such as *then, after, before, finally* and also phrases such as *in the morning, during the storm, after the rain,* and *at lunchtime*.

Read *Wednesday and Ruby* to the class. Have students identify the time words in the text. Some of these will be phrases and some will be adverbs. Students do not need to give these grammatical labels at this stage. They simply need to understand how to sequence events through time in their own stories and recounts and how to identify the passage of time in texts they are reading or listening to.

Different types of texts have different ways of expressing the passage of time. Procedural texts usually have a logical sequence using numbers or steps. Explanations often use connectives that show time and cause (for example, *then, after that, so that, because*) to show sequence.

Grammar Focus: Contractions, alliteration
Type of Text: Persuasive – Exposition/Advertisement

Student Book 1
Unit 26

Talk to students about advertising and its function to sell things. Ask students to suggest television advertisements that they like or dislike. Ask students which advertisements make them want to buy a product. Make a list of things that students like about the ads: music, dancing, songs, images, colours, what is said or claimed about what the product can do, famous people using the product, the use of animals or characters such as clowns, children making recommendations, or photos of the product looking really tasty or really cool.

Hold up a classroom item such as a biro or picture book. Ask students what they could say about the item if they were trying to sell it, for example: *This biro works really well. This biro will last for months and not run out. This biro is very comfortable to hold so you won't get a tired hand. It will help you do your homework.* Ask volunteers to make a 'sales pitch' to the class using a persuasive voice.

Alliteration is about repeated sounds at the beginning of words: *crispy crunchy corn cookies*. Onomatopoeia, introduced in Unit 25, is also about the sounds of words. Rich-sounding words add interest in ads, poetry, drama and narratives. Alliteration and onomatopoeia would not usually be appropriate in factual texts such as information reports or explanations. Ask your school's teacher/librarian to find books available in your school that make use of these language features. Some may also include rhyme.

Create some class tongue twisters that make use of alliteration and onomatopoeia. Illustrate and display the tongue twisters. Have students practise saying them swiftly.

Teach students about contractions, particularly *it's (it is)* and *you'll (you will)*.

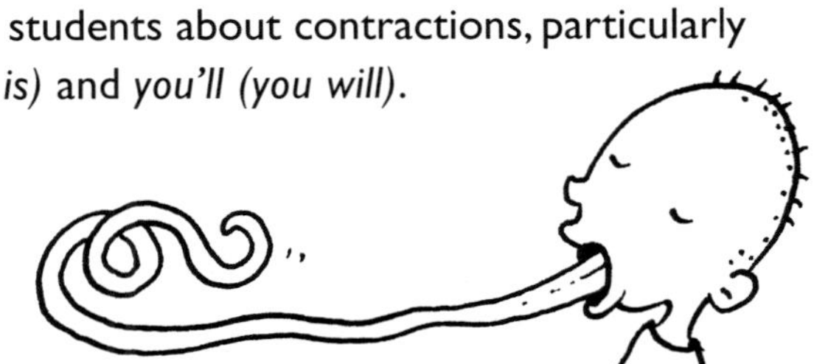

Grammar Focus: Thinking and feeling verbs, antonyms
Type of Text: Persuasive – Exposition

Student Book 1 **Unit 27**

This text, *Sharks*, presents one person's opinion about sharks. The opinion is supported with reasons that state why the shark is the person's favourite animal.

Draw an outline of a person's head. Around the person's head, write thinking and feeling verbs *(think, believe, hate, love, imagine, hope, want, know, like, feel)*. Point out to students that these words help to present opinions and arguments. Tell them we can't see these verbs happening the way we can see doing verbs like *jumping* or *eating*. Thinking and feeling verbs take place inside our brains. Ask students to use the verbs in sentences of their own to present opinions about sharks or their own favourite animals.

Model the construction of an argument text for students. Write only one side of the argument and use thinking and feeling verbs to present the opinions and reasons.

You might have discussed antonyms with students in Unit 14 if you read them *Where is the Green Sheep?* by Mem Fox and Judy Horacek (Penguin). Point out that sometimes antonyms can be made by adding or changing a few letters in front of a word (prefixes):

happy → *unhappy*   *respect* → *disrespect*
understand → *misunderstand*

Antonyms can also be made by adding or changing a few letters at the end of a word (suffixes):

harmful → *harmless*   *thoughtful* → *thoughtless*

Create word banks of antonyms.

Display comic strips and cartoons that include thought balloons to tell what a person is thinking or feeling. Use sticky notes in Big Book narratives to write the thoughts and feelings of characters. In stories, thinking and feeling verbs help readers to know how a character is feeling. This helps the reader to empathise with characters. Explain the concept of empathy to students as 'putting yourself in their shoes'.

Grammar Focus: How words
Type of Text: Informative – Procedure/Instructions

Student Book 1 **Unit 28**

Read the fairytale *Cinderella* to the class in case some students are not familiar with the tale. This will support their understanding of the tongue-in-cheek humour in *Cinderfella's Jobs*.

Cinderfella's Jobs is a set of instructions for Cinderfella. Point out to students that Cinderfella is a male Cinderella and the text is having fun with the fairytale by switching genders.

Read the instructions *Cinderfella's Jobs* with students. Talk about the commands. These are the actions that Cinderfella is required to do: clean, mop, scrub, make, wash. Remind students of the way commands were written in Units 9 and 17: with a doing verb at the start of each command. Ask students to identify and read the words in front of each doing verb: *quietly, spotlessly, briskly, neatly, carefully.* Point out that each of these words tells how to do the action. These can be called 'how words' because they tell 'how' to do something. Give students further examples of how words in commands.

Quietly sit down.

Quickly stand up.

Carefully jump on the spot.

Carefully write in the columns.

Read your books silently.

Cheer enthusiastically for your team.

Add how words to the command *Walk to my desk: Slowly walk to my desk/noisily, quickly, lazily, cheekily, sneakily, laughingly*. Have individual students role-play the walks to the desk according to the how word used.

Question 3 asks students to write their opinions and support the opinions with reasons. Remind them they need to remember to use thinking and feeling verbs.

Read other fairytales to the class and display them in the classroom. Allow students to work in pairs or small groups to complete the **Try it yourself!** activity, if this is appropriate.

Grammar Focus: Number adjectives
Type of Text: Informative – Procedure/Recipe

Student Book 1
Unit 29

Read the *Magic Potion* recipe with students. Ask students to tell you what they notice about the recipe. They might suggest that it has a list of ingredients; it tells you what to do (the Method); it has commands; it has doing verbs; the commands are written in number order; the commands all start with a verb.

Point out to students the number words in the ingredients list. These are adjectives. They describe quantities of things. Recipes usually include number adjectives to describe quantities of ingredients. Make sure students realise that in a real recipe it is very important to have exact number adjectives otherwise the recipe will not work out. Teach students the difference between cardinal numbers *(one, two, three, fifty)* and ordinal numbers *(first, second, third, fiftieth)*. Tell students that number adjectives are also words that tell inexact quantities such as <u>some</u> *sauce,* <u>any</u> *gift.*

Display recipes and cookbooks in the classroom. Point out that recipes often include pictures or photographs so that people can see what the finished product should look like.

Read picture books that involve recipes, potions, magic spells or magic ingredients such as:

Possum Magic written by Mem Fox and illustrated by Julie Vivas (Omnibus). Point out the use of alliteration.

Wombat Stew written by Marcia K Vaughan and illustrated by Pamela Lofts (Scholastic). This narrative makes use of rhyme as well as alliteration.

Collate the magic recipes students write for the **Try it Yourself!** activity as a class book and make it available for students to read in class time.

Grammar Focus: Compound words
Type of Text: Informative – Explanation/Cycle diagram

Student Book 1
Unit 31

Life cycles are often explained in cycle diagrams. They are called cycles because they form a circle. The life cycle keeps starting over again as babies are born and then have their own babies in the circle of life. Explain this concept to students and then read and examine the diagram and explanation in Unit 31. Point out the technical terminology that is relevant to the explanation. Display factual books and posters that show life cycles, especially insects and mini-beasts.

Photocopy and distribute **Reproducible 1** (page 75), which includes a word cloze of doing verbs for students to complete. When completed the text can then be used for jigsaw cloze (see page 13 for instructions on cloze).

Make sure students understand the rule on compound words. A compound word is a word formed from two smaller words.

Create a class word bank of compound words, such as: *everywhere, sometimes, everyone, anyone, somebody, anybody, maybe*, as well as the compound words included in the unit: *softball, football, bathroom, bedroom, Sunday, birthday*.

Display and discuss the cycle diagrams completed for the **Try it yourself!** activity.

Grammar Focus: Phrases that tell where
Type of Text: Informative – Procedure/Directions

Student Book 1
Unit 32

Read students tales of *Red Riding Hood, Goldilocks and the Three Bears, the Three Billy Goats Gruff, Hansel and Gretel, Rapunzel* and *Ding Dong Dell*, so that they can appreciate the references to the story characters in *How to Get Home*.

Read the map and directions with students. The directions are commands that all start with a doing verb. Point this out to students. Tell them that directions tell where to go. Ask volunteers to give oral directions to their homes from the school gate. Talk to students about the importance of giving directions in the correct sequence and what would happen if you gave directions in an incorrect sequence – people would get lost.

Have students dramatise the journey *How to Get Home*. Characters hiding in the story map can speak as the little bear walks past them.

Tell students that groups of words that tell where things happen in a story are called 'where phrases': *in the paddock, under a bridge, behind the tree, on the roof, in a tower.* Ask students to orally suggest a where phrase for a place in your school or classroom. Ask students to listen out for where phrases in stories you read to them.

Have students suggest a how word to add to the front of each command in *How to Get Home*.

Have students create pirate treasure maps and write directions using commands and where phrases to find the treasure.

Model how to create a story map for a book you are reading to the class. Mark the character's journey, or the place of each incident in the story, on the map.

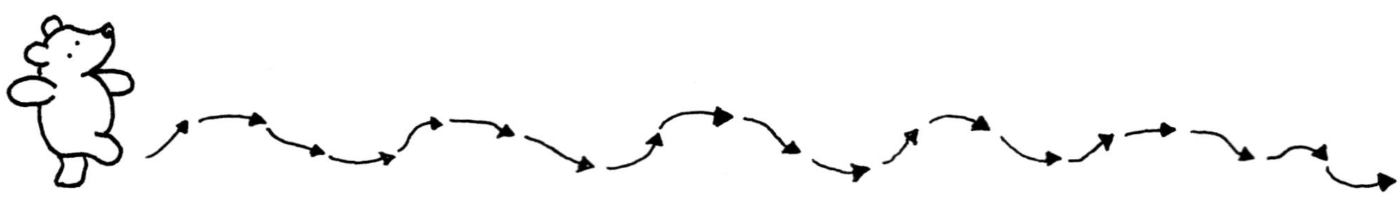

Grammar Focus: Speech marks
Type of Text: Persuasive – Response/Book review

Student Book 1
Unit 33

Use Big Books that include dialogue between characters to teach students how to use speech marks. Have students read the characters' speech in the Big Books or perform the stories as Readers' Theatre (see page 18 for instructions on Readers' Theatre). You can read the rest of the text yourself as the narrator.

The *Book Review* is a response text. It tells the writer's response to a book called *The Bunyip of Berkeley's Creek* (Penguin). Read the book to the class if it is available in your school. Ask students for their response to the story. Remind them to give opinions with supporting reasons.

Talk to students about the bunyip's feelings. Ask students to identify adjectives used in the story to describe the bunyip and comments that each animal makes about the bunyip's appearance. Ask students to identify questions and exclamations in the story and in the *Book Review*.

Students might enjoy creating a large poster-sized painting of a bunyip for the classroom wall, and writing the speech of the animals in the story on labels to display with the bunyip, for example: *"They have horrible tails and even more horrible fur," said the emu.* Label the poster *"What do bunyips look like?" asked the bunyip.* Focus students' attention on the punctuation marks for the questions and statements as well as the speech marks. Use the book to point out the saying verbs to students: *called, asked, replied, considered, said, sighed, murmured, shouted.*

Use Big Books and sticky notes to add speech balloons and thought bubbles to illustrations of characters.

Grammar Focus: Repeated words
Type of Text: Informative – Information report

Student Book 1
Unit 34

Read *Koalas* with students. Talk to students about the structure of the text and the types of information included in the text. It tells:

- what koalas are
- where they can be found
- what they look like
- what they eat
- things they do
- noises they make.

Ask students to identify the nouns and adjectives used to label koalas and describe aspects of their appearance and habits. Make sure that students understand that the information is factual. Ask students to offer their opinions about koalas and ensure they recognise the difference.

Help students to recognise word chains for reference (reference chains) in *Koalas*. Point out the nouns and the pronouns that refer to the nouns: *koalas/they*.

Point out other ways to keep track of nouns. For example, through words that point out: *Koalas scream. Their scream . . .*; and through ellipsis: *Koalas sleep in the day and [koalas/they] are active at night.*

Photocopy **Reproducible 2** (page 76) for students to complete in pairs. It is a word cloze activity for pronouns.

Model how to construct an information report. Research an animal. Collect and record information in categories, columns, or in a semantic web (see page 14 for an explanation of semantic webs). Point out that the information is factual.

Revise exclamation marks and speech marks. Use **Reproducible 10** on page 84.

Student Book 2

Scope and Sequence

This scope and sequence chart is based on the requirements of the Australian Curriculum.

Unit	Unit name/ Type of text	Clause to whole text level			Word and word group level		
		Sentences and clauses	Cohesion: theme, pronouns, lexical chains, connectives	Mood and modality, language and vocabulary	Nouns and noun groups	Verbs and verb groups	Adverbs and prepositional phrases
1	**Life Cycle of a Bird** Explanation/Cycle diagram				common nouns		
2	**Come to My Party!** Information report/ Invitation				proper nouns; common nouns		
3	**Move It!** Description/Poem				common nouns; proper nouns	doing verbs	
4	**Sloths** Information report	sentences; full stops and capital letters			common nouns; proper nouns	doing verbs	
5	**Flies** Information report/ Conversation	quoted speech; speech marks			proper nouns	saying verbs; doing verbs	
6	REVISION						
7	**Children's Python** Description	sentences			describing adjectives; common nouns; proper nouns	doing verbs	
8	**The Best Pet** Exposition			antonyms	common nouns; describing adjectives	thinking and feeling verbs; doing verbs	
9	**Dear Gran and Pa** Recount/Letter	quoted speech	connectives		nouns	verbs	
10	**Bee** Information report/ Diagram	sentences			common nouns	being and having verbs	
11	**Freddy and His Egg** Narrative		synonyms; antonyms	onomatopoeia	nouns; adjectives	doing verbs; thinking and feeling verbs	
12	REVISION						
13	**The Secret Ingredient** Procedure/Instructions	quoted speech; speech marks		commands	common nouns	doing verbs	
14	**Lost Dog** Information report/ Map	quoted speech		compound words; commands	adjectives	doing verbs	
15	**A Loony Cat** Description		personal pronouns	compound words	common nouns	doing verbs; saying verbs	
16	**How** Description/Poem	sentences			singular and plural nouns	verbs	adverbs to tell how
17	**Hypnotic** Response/Art review		personal pronouns		adjectives; common nouns		
18	REVISION						

Unit	Unit name/ Type of text	Clause to whole text level			Word and word group level		
		Sentences and clauses	Cohesion: theme, pronouns, lexical chains, connectives	Mood and modality, language and vocabulary	Nouns and noun groups	Verbs and verb groups	Adverbs and prepositional phrases
19	**Giant Pandas** Response				noun groups; nouns; adjectives		
20	**Wildlife Carer** Interview/Questions and answers			questions; statements; fact and opinion			
21	**Where's My Mum?** Narrative			fact and opinion	common nouns		prepositions to tell where
22	**Along Came a Spider** Narrative	quoted speech; sentences	personal pronouns	exclamations; questions	nouns; adjectives		
23	**Llamas for Sale!** Advertisement		connectives	emotive words	noun groups		
24	REVISION						
25	**Zoos** Discussion	reported and quoted speech; paragraphs	connectives	point of view			
26	**How Do Baby Penguins Eat?** Explanation			questions	noun groups		
27	**Reptile Encounter** Recount		connectives	contractions	noun groups		adverbs to tell when
28	**'Talk to the Animals' Potion** Procedure/Recipe			commands; alliteration; rhyme; emotive words		doing verbs	
29	**Ringtail Possums** Information report	phrases	connectives		noun groups		prepositions and prepositional phrases to tell where and when
30	REVISION						
31	**Corroboree Frogs** Information report		lexical chains		noun groups	being and having verbs	prepositional phrases to tell where
32	**The Chimp and the Crocodile** Narrative/Fable				noun groups; proper nouns	verb tense; past tense verbs	
33	**How to Look After a Tarantula** Procedure/Instructions	sentences		commands	plural nouns; common nouns; proper nouns	verbs	
34	**How Sea Animals Breathe** Explanation	sentences	connectives			doing verbs	
35	REVISION						

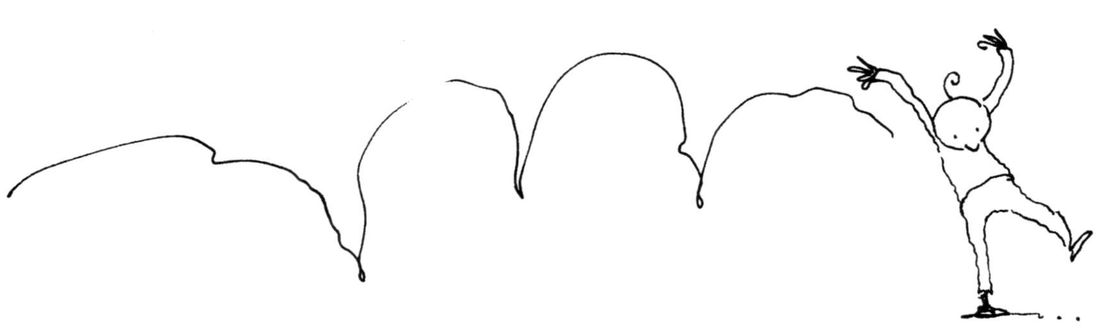

Grammar Focus: Common nouns
Type of Text: Informative – Explanation/Cycle diagram

Student Book 2 **Unit 1**

Life Cycle of a Bird is an explanation text. Explanations explain a sequence of events in logical or chronological order. Explanations often make use of diagrams and illustration. A cycle diagram is used to show the circle of life. Point out the function of the cycle diagram to students. The diagram shows the significant events in a bird's life in sequence.

The unit focuses on common nouns. Tell students to remember that '***n**ouns **n**ame*' things by remembering that both words start with ***n***. At this stage students can focus on concrete nouns (nouns for things that can be seen, heard or touched) rather than abstract nouns (nouns for something that cannot be seen, heard or touched; for example an emotion like *sadness*, or a concept like *peace*). Label things in the classroom with common noun labels: *desk, window, door, chair, plant, fish tank, jar, cupboard* and so on.

Play a game of 'Snap' with matching pairs of common nouns (see page 17 for instructions).

Brainstorm lists in categories and create word banks of common nouns related to other learning areas. Students can refer to these word banks for their own writing and spelling. Play 'I Spy' to name nouns beginning with letters or sounds, for example *I spy with my little eye a noun beginning with 't' (teacher)*.

Use words from the deck of 'Snap' cards to practise placing nouns in alphabetical order and to practise dictionary use.

Display and discuss students' life cycle diagrams completed for the **Try it yourself!** activity.

Grammar Focus: Proper nouns
Type of Text: Informative – Information report/Invitation

Student Book 2 **Unit 2**

Discuss birthdays and their significance for students in your class. Ask if birthdays are celebrated in any special ways, with families or friends. Recognise that some families are busy with work and have financial commitments that cannot support expensive birthday parties. Read *Come to My Party* with students. Talk about parties that people have for other significant occasions such as weddings, or religious and cultural festivals. Have students share their knowledge of these parties and discuss food, music, gift-giving and other traditions that they remember about the parties.

Talk to students about nouns that are called 'proper' because they are the important names of people or particular places. Tell students that all proper nouns start with a capital letter, including names for people, places, books, films, days and months.

Write the days of the week and the months of the year on charts for students to refer to in their writing. Have students recite the days of the week in chronological order. Make sure students recognise the chronological sequence of the months of the year.

Write the proper noun first names of students in the class. Create a birthday chart for students in the class to show the months of their birth.

Role-play a 'posh' tea party. Have students select one prop each from a props box – for example, a hat, scarf, fake jewellery, tie, umbrella, cane or feather boa. Tell students to think of proper noun names for themselves in character. Write some alliterative proper noun names on the board as examples, such as *Lady Lillian, Sir Stanley Stanton*. Then have them form pairs and introduce each other to other pairs, using 'posh' accents, as they walk around the room: *"How do you do?" "Pleased to meet you." "This is my friend__________."* Come together as a whole class and discuss students' responses to the tea party role-play.

Grammar Focus: Doing verbs
Type of Text: Imaginative – Description/Poem

Student Book 2 **Unit 3**

Tell students that some words are used to refer to an action. These are called doing verbs.

Read the poem with students. Discuss the doing verbs *(leap, hop, jump, swim, watch, crawl, dive, roll, swoop, fly, soar, glide, slither, slide, curl, sleep)*. Organise a display of books that show animals and describe animal actions and behaviours.

Brainstorm a list of common nouns for animals in alphabetical order: *alligator, bee, chimpanzee* and so on (z could stand for *zoo animals*). Have students work in pairs to think of a doing verb for what each animal can do. Encourage students to use dictionaries and thesauruses to think of interesting words. Compile the doing verbs onto one chart. Allocate an animal to each student or pair of students in the class. Have them create a page for a class animal alphabet book.

Trace around the body of a student in the class and then cut out, paint and decorate the body. Brainstorm doing verbs for actions the body can do, such as *eat, jump, hop, run, leap* and *swim*.

Display the doing verbs with the body. If students name saying verbs or thinking and feeling verbs at this stage, it is not necessary to specify the differences between the different kinds of verbs. The distinction can be learnt as students progress through the student book. Focus instead on the doing aspect of all verbs.

Add extra stanzas to the poem *Move It!* Have students recite the poem as a Multi-voice Recitation and perform for a school assembly (see page 18 for instructions on Multi-voice Recitation).

Grammar Focus: Sentences
Type of Text: Informative – Information report

Student Book 2 **Unit 4**

Read *Sloths* with the class. Ask students to identify any aspects of grammar that they have noticed about the text. They should notice common and proper nouns as well as some doing verbs for what sloths do.

The text is an information report. It includes an opening statement and then information about aspects of a sloth's life. Talk to students about the categories of information provided in the report: what sloths are, where they live, what they look like, what they eat, what eats them, what they do, how they move.

Talk to students about sentences. Tell students that sentences need to make sense and that they always start with a capital letter. Tell students that sentences in information reports end in full stops. Focus students' attention on the full stops and capital letters in *Sloths*. The text consists of nine sentences. Reinforce the idea of a sentence: ask nine students to read a sentence each in turn.

Have students each choose an animal, or work in pairs to choose an animal to research for the **Try it yourself!** activity. Tell them to research the following about their animal: where they can be found, what they look like, what they eat, things they do and noises they make. Have students then use this information to construct an information report to share with the rest of the class.

Conduct sentence cloze with sentences written by students for each other. Have students write sentences. Check their punctuation and grammar to ensure they have actually written full sentences. Tell them to cut their sentence into separate words. Place each sentence in an envelope or container of its own. A challenge for gifted students is to mix two separate typed sentences in the one envelope and have students work out the two from the jumble.

Grammar Focus: Saying verbs
Type of Text: Informative and Persuasive – Information report/Conversation

Student Book 2
Unit 5

Flies is a conversation. Choose two students to read what Jessica says and what Bob says (the quoted speech) in the conversation. Read the rest of the text yourself as a narrator, or choose another student to be the narrator and highlight the narrator's lines *(announced Jessica; said Bob; replied Jessica; stated Bob)*. Point out the speech marks that are used to mark what the two children say in their conversation. Point out the saying verbs that are used to indicate something is being said. You might also like to point out the exclamation *Erk!* Exclamations and speech marks will be dealt with later in the student book.

Use the term 'quoted speech' to label what a person actually says. Use Big Books and picture books to show students examples of quoted speech. Ask your school's teacher/librarian to find samples for you. Books such as *Owl Babies* by Martin Waddell and illustrated by Patrick Benson (Walker Books) provide examples of speech marks, saying verbs and exclamations.

Demonstrate for students how to record conversation using speech marks and saying verbs. Books such as *Owl Babies* would be suitable for Readers' Theatre presentations, where characters' lines are allocated to students to read and another one or two students read the lines of the narrator (see page 18 for instructions on Readers' Theatre).

Conduct cloze activities using Big Books that include dialogue. Cover the saying verbs with sticky notes and ask students to suggest suitable saying verbs. Read the dialogue in the ways indicated by the saying verbs.

Make a class book of animal sentences, using quoted speech and saying verbs.

"I'm hungry," <u>hooted</u> the baby owl.

Grammar Focus: Describing adjectives
Type of Text: Informative – Description

Student Book 2
Unit 7

Children's Python is a description text. It describes a child's pet snake. Talk to students about the structure of the text. It begins with an orientation to say whose pet it is. Then it describes what the snake looks like and feels like, and how it behaves. The text ends with a summing-up opinion or conclusion, which is the writer's personal opinion about the snake. Ask students what that opinion is.

Point out the full stops and capital letters in the text, which indicate ten sentences. Have ten students read a sentence each in turn out loud to the class.

Ask students to suggest words of their own or words from the text that describe Molly the snake: gentle, beautiful, quiet. These words can describe the snake's texture, size colour, shape, movement, personality and so on. Point out to students that adjectives can be factual *(brown)* or they can give an opinion *(beautiful)*.

Use a Big Book to demonstrate the function of adjectives to describe. Cover the adjectives with sticky notes. Read the story to students and ask them to suggest alternative adjectives. They can use illustrations and the story context to predict appropriate adjectives. The ones suggested might be the adjectives in the text or they might be synonyms for the actual adjectives used in the story. Write students' suggestions on the sticky notes. Compare the story results.

Point out the word *she* in the text. Tell students that *she* refers to the female snake, Molly. Read the text saying 'Molly' for each *she*. Make sure students recognise that using Molly for every reference to the snake makes the text very repetitive.

Grammar Focus: Thinking and feeling verbs
Type of Text: Persuasive – Exposition

Student Book 2 **Unit 8**

The Best Pet presents one person's opinion about the best pet. Read the text with students. Ask students to state the reasons the writer gives for thinking mice make the best pets. Ask students if they have had mice as pets and what they thought about mice as pets. Make sure students understand that exposition texts give opinions but that opinions need to be supported by reasons. In other words, it is important to be able to justify your opinions.

Point out to students that we use thinking and feeling verbs when we give our opinions about something. We use verbs such as *I think that . . . , We believe that . . ., My mum feels that . . ., My dad loves . . .* Add sticky notes to the illustrations of characters in picture books that you are reading with the class. Use Big Books so that students can clearly see the writing. Create thought balloons on the sticky notes. Express what the characters are thinking and feeling. Use thinking and feeling verbs. *Where the Wild Things Are* by Maurice Sendak (Red Fox) would be suitable for adding a thought balloon for Max to each page.

Have students present their expositions created for the **Try it yourself!** activity as spoken texts to the class. Tell them to use voice, facial expression and body language to sound very convinced and determined that their choice of pet is the best pet to have.

Ask students to suggest an antonym for every adjective in the *Best Pet* so that it becomes *The Worst Pet*. Discuss the difference made to the text. Brainstorm a class list of adjectives and their antonyms. Create a word bank. Create a deck of cards with matching pairs of antonyms to use for Snap or Concentration games (see page 17 and 16 for instructions on Snap and Concentration).

Grammar Focus: Connectives
Type of Text: Informative – Recount/Letter

Student Book 2 **Unit 9**

Recounts tell of events that have already occurred. Recounts retell these events in the time order that they happened. Read *Dear Gran and Pa* with students. Ask students to identify the doing verbs. Point out the forms of the verbs in the letter. The verbs help to tell the reader that the events happened in the past *(went, asked, said, decided)*. Point out the other words that help to sequence the letter in time *(yesterday, first, then, finally, next Sunday)*.

Jointly construct a recount with the class that retells a series of events that have occurred. For example: *This morning we walked to the library for our lesson. On the way to the library we saw the principal and said good morning. Then we . . . After that we . . .* Focus students' attention on the words that tell time order and the use of past tense verb forms.

Connectives are joining words that join one part of a sentence or text with another part. Connectives can join in time *(then, after, when)* or through cause or reason *(so, because, but)*. The word *and* is also a connective. It joins parts of sentences by adding them on. *I like dogs and I like cats*. Or, *I like dogs and cats*.

Help students create sentences orally that use the connectives *first, next, after, so, but, because, since, finally, firstly.* For example:

We like ____________ because ______________.
(connective that shows cause)

We'll do __________ after we finish __________.
(connective that shows time)

Have students work in pairs to draw storyboards or cartoon strips that show the sequence of events described in the letter.

Compare and discuss students' answers for question 5.

Grammar Focus: Being and having verbs
Type of Text: Informative – Information report/Diagram

Student Book 2 **Unit 10**

The diagram *Bee* gives information about the body parts of a bee. Information report texts are often accompanied by diagrams and illustrations. Their function is to make the information easier to understand. Discuss the body parts of a bee that make it the same as other insects, and the body parts that make it different from other insects.

Display factual books and posters about bees and insects for students to particularly examine the illustrations, diagrams and photographs.

Tell students that being and having verbs show what things are and what things have. For example:

Bees are insects.

Bees have six legs.

Other being and having verbs include: *is, am, are, was, were, has, have, had.* Ask students to suggest sentences that make use of these being and having verbs.

Have students draw a diagram of an insect other than a bee and label its body parts. They could draw an ant, a cicada, a praying mantis, a cockroach or any other insect. They should use the books on display in the classroom for their research. Tell students to write a few sentences to describe the insect using being and having verbs. Provide them with a format, if necessary. For example:

This is a ____________________.

It has ____________________.

It has ____________________.

Display and discuss students' diagrams.

Grammar Focus: Nouns, onomatopoeia
Type of Text: Imaginative – Narrative

Student Book 2 **Unit 11**

Talk about the structure of narrative texts. Narratives need an orientation that introduces the story's characters, either human or animal. Then they need some action or something to happen to the characters. This is called the complication. The complication can be one problem or a series of problems. Then narratives need an ending where the characters overcome their problems.

Read *Freddy and His Egg* with students. Ask students to identify the main character, as well as the orientation and complication.

Display and share a range of narrative books with the class. Ask students to name the characters in individual stories with which they are familiar. Ask them to retell what happens to the characters. What problems do the characters face? How do the characters overcome their problems? Have students select a picture book or other form of narrative text from the display in the classroom. Have them identify the main character, the setting and the complication in their narrative.

Talk to students about onomatopoeia (words that sound like the thing they represent). Poetry and narratives often include onomatopoeia to make them sound more exciting or interesting. Scary stories might include onomatopoeia for creaky doors and eerie howling. Find examples of onomatopoeia in narratives and poetry to share with the class.

Organise a Multi-voice Recitation of nature poems and add your own onomatopoeic words as background noise for wind, rain and storms (see page 18 for instructions on Multi-voice Recitation). Poems about food could include a chorus of gobbling, lip-smacking and slurping sounds.

What's that Noise? by Mary Roennfeldt and illustrated by Robert Roennfeldt (Omnibus) is an example of a picture book that makes use of animal sounds represented in onomatopoeic words.

Collate students' stories for the **Try it yourself!** activity as a class book.

Grammar Focus: Commands
Type of Text: Informative – Procedure/Instructions

Student Book 2
Unit 13

The Secret Ingredient is a procedure text. It gives instructions to find something in a backyard. Read the text with the class. The steps in the instructions are written as commands. Commands tell you what to do to achieve the goal. Commands often begin with a verb. *<u>Pack</u> that away. <u>Tidy</u> your room.* Point out the doing verbs at the start of each command in *The Secret Ingredient: Hop, Step, Crawl, Find, Dig, Examine, Return.*

Identify with students the locations they will need to draw on their maps of the backyard: a big tree and a flower bed. It will not matter where exactly they draw these on their maps. Then they need to mark a route on their maps. Provide time for students to share their maps with others in the class.

Talk about the way a person can use voice and facial expression to give commands. Have students work in pairs. Tell them to take turns giving each other commands. Have one member of each pair be a teacher and the other a child. Tell the teachers to be really bossy and command the child 'Do your work', 'Sit down', 'Stand up', 'Walk to the door'. Swap roles. Have 'teachers' now give commands in a 'not bossy' way. Discuss the differences made by voice, facial expression and body language to the way a command is given and received.

Question 5 requires students to create sentences incorporating quoted speech. Revise the use of speech marks and saying verbs so that they punctuate their answers correctly. Brainstorm the sorts of commands issued at home and to a dog before students attempt to write their sentences.

Grammar Focus: Compound words, adjectives
Type of Text: Informative – Information report/Map

Student Book 2
Unit 14

Have students examine the map for *Lost Dog*. Ask students what they know about maps and street directories and what they notice about this map.

Some picture books include story maps. Read *Queenie and the Bantam* for example, by Bob Graham (Walker Books). It includes a location map. Ask your school's teacher/librarian to find books with story maps and examine these with students. Display street directories and allow time for students to examine them and find their own addresses and the school.

Demonstrate for students how to create story maps for picture books that involve a journey or include specific points of a location. For example, *Zoo* by Anthony Browne (Red Fox), describes a family's visit to a zoo. Students could create a map of the zoo in the story and then write directions for the route the family took to see the animals and mark their route on the map. Remind students that instructions and directions are commands and that commands usually start with doing verbs.

Create a class list of compound words: *breakfast, Sunday, somebody, anyone, football, classroom, fingernail, kneecap, headache, homework, everybody, something, grandparent, sunscreen, handbag, bookcase, hairbrush, armchair, playground, supermarket, bookstore, desktop, fingertip* and so on.

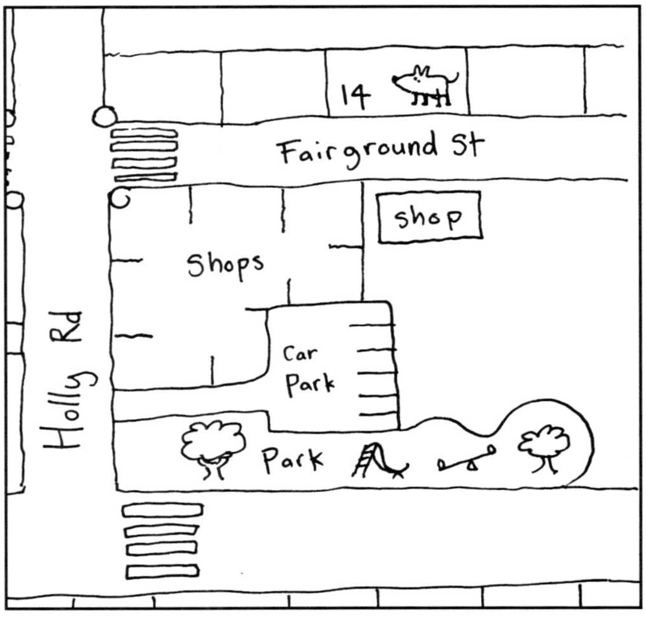

Grammar Focus: Personal pronouns
Type of Text: Informative – Description

Student Book 2 **Unit 15**

Read *A Loony Cat* with students. Discuss the meaning of the term 'loony' as a colloquial form of 'lunatic'. Demonstrate for students how to use a thesaurus to find synonyms for loony, such as *crazy, nutty, silly, batty, balmy, foolish, madcap, mad.* Ask students about their pets and any 'loony' things their animals do.

Talk about animal antics students have seen in films and on television shows, including cartoons. Choose an animal 'star' that students are familiar with, such as an animated animal from a popular children's movie, or an animal hero from a children's book. Jointly construct an award for the animal, which students can use as a model for the awards they create for the **Try it yourself!** activity.

Talk to students about personal pronouns. These words replace nouns for people and things: *me, I, we, us, you, he, him, she, her, it, they, them*. Point out to students that it makes a text easier to follow when pronouns are used properly. Give them examples such as:

The children ate lunch and then the children played in the park.

The children ate lunch and then they played in the park.

Point out also that sometimes pronouns make texts confusing. For example:

Ali talked to Susie on the telephone and she wasn't happy.

We can't tell which girl was unhappy. The sentence can be written more clearly:

Ali talked to Susie on the telephone and Susie wasn't happy.

Ali wasn't happy when she talked to Susie on the telephone.

Another example would be:

The dog ran after the ball. It got muddy.

We don't know whether the dog got muddy or the ball, because the writing is not really clear. Make sure students understand how important it is that pronouns clearly refer to particular nouns.

Grammar Focus: Adverbs
Type of Text: Imaginative – Description/Poem

Student Book 2 **Unit 16**

Point out the structure of the poem *How*. Each sentence consists of: a common noun for an animal; a verb for what it does; a 'how' adverb to add meaning to the verb by telling *how* the verb is done; and a phrase that tells *how* or *where*.

Cats	*creep*	*quietly*	*on soft pads.*
common noun	verb	how	how
animal name		adverb	phrase

Woodpeckers	*knock*	*loudly*	*on the trunks of trees.*
common noun	verb	how	where
animal name		adverb	phrase

Jointly construct extra stanzas for the poem by following the same grammatical pattern.

Organise a Multi-voice Recitation of the poem (see page 18 for instructions on Multi-voice Recitation).

The poem could also be collated into a class book. Have students add extra pages for animals they write about.

Tell students to remember what adverbs are by saying they add meaning to verbs.

add + verb = adverb

Point out to students that sometimes commands make use of adverbs to tell 'how' to follow the command *Quietly sit/Sit quietly*.

Discuss the spelling rules for singular and plural nouns. Make a poster for display in the classroom that students can refer to when they need help with plural and singular nouns. Create 'plural words' word banks, including words that end in *–s* or –es, words that change their middle letters to form the plural, such as *man/men*, and words that do not change for plural, such as *sheep/sheep*.

Grammar Focus: Adjectives
Type of Text: Persuasive – Response/Art review

Student Book 2 **Unit 17**

Hypnotic is a response to a painting of a leopard. Discuss students' answers to question 2 (the definition of 'hypnotic' and why the painting is named *Hypnotic*). Discuss the use of adjectives to describe the leopard and the painting.

Display books and photographs of animals for the students to examine. Tell students to choose one animal and create an artwork to represent it. Allow students to use crayons, felt-tip pens, pencils and paint. They should then write a label for the painting that includes a name for the artwork and reasons why they chose the animal and painted it in the way they did. For example:

'Mud Beast' by Amrin

I painted a hippo in the mud because it looked happy. I used a lot of muddy brown paint and I made the hippo's eyes white.

Display students' paintings and then ask students to give responses to the artworks. Start them off by modelling a response of your own.

For example *I like the painting of the hippo because the hippo is covered in so much mud you can really only see its eyes. I think it is enjoying itself.*

Encourage students to comment about any of the paintings and not just the paintings completed by their friends.

Provide students with sticky notes and have them write adjectives to display with the paintings: *muddy, happy, brown.*

Students can start to learn to recognise the different kinds of adjectives and their function in texts: number adjectives, describing adjectives and classifying adjectives.

Grammar Focus: Noun groups
Type of Text: Persuasive – Response

Student Book 2 **Unit 19**

Spend some time talking with students about adjectives: number adjectives, describing adjectives and classifying adjectives. These words, when placed with a noun, form groups of words that are called noun groups. Students should be quite familiar with describing adjectives. Number adjectives are fairly easy to recognise. Classifying adjectives are a little more difficult to differentiate because they are often nouns in their own right.

I watched the <u>tennis</u>. (*tennis* is a noun here)

I watched the <u>tennis</u> match. (*tennis* is a classifying adjective here – it classifies the type of match)

Make sure that students recognise that classifying adjectives are words that classify or categorise the noun.

<u>gum</u> tree, <u>kelpie</u> dog, <u>homework</u> book, <u>Italian</u> food, <u>football</u> game

Make a chart for display in the classroom. For example:

A noun group includes a noun and words that tell more about the noun:

	noun group			
We played	*<u>three</u>*	*<u>long</u>*	*<u>softball</u>*	*<u>games</u>.*
	number adjective	describing adjective	classifying adjective	noun

Words that show ownership can also be part of the noun group. These words are sometimes called possessive adjectives.

noun group			
<u>Our</u>	*<u>five</u>*	*<u>puppies</u>*	*are very noisy.*
word to show ownership	number adjective	noun	

Read *Giant Pandas* with students. Ask students to identify words in the text that are part of noun groups. Revise the personal pronouns *he, they,* and *I* and have students identify them in the text.

Have students work in pairs to make dioramas of real or imaginary animals in the wild. A diorama is a scene in a box. Tell them to add labels to the scene.

Grammar Focus: Questions and statements
Type of Text: Informative – Interview/Questions and answers

Student Book 2 **Unit 20**

Wildlife Carer is an interview. It begins with an orientation and then includes questions and answers.

Remind students that sentences start with capital letters.

Tell students that questions are sentences that ask something. Questions end with question marks rather than full stops.

Answers are usually statements. They are sentences that give information and/or opinions. Answers end in full stops.

Write the words *who, what, where, when, how, why* on a chart for student reference. Tell students that these are useful question starter words. Play Hot Seat and have students be interviewed by other class members (see page 17 for instructions on Hot Seat). Students can pretend to be story characters, someone they know, a television character or someone working in a particular occupation.

Have students use the question starter words to ask questions of the person in the Hot Seat.

If appropriate, investigate the work of organisations in your area that assist sick or orphaned native animals. It might be possible for a volunteer to visit your school and talk about the work of the organisation. Prepare interview questions with the class prior to any visit by a guest speaker.

Talk to students about the difference between facts and opinions. Create a chart that has two columns labelled *Fact* and *Opinion*. Have students write a fact and an opinion onto strips of paper and attach the paper to the chart columns. Allow them to use the factual books on display in the classroom to find facts.

Grammar Focus: Prepositions
Type of Text: Imaginative – Narrative

Student Book 2 **Unit 21**

Read the narrative *Where's My Mum?* with students. Organise students to perform the narrative as a play. Choose students to be the duckling and each of the other animals in the narrative. Then have the duckling ask the question of each animal in sequence: *"Cow, have you seen my mother? Horse, have you seen my mother?"* and so on. Have each animal respond to the question appropriately. The students can create their own dialogue. Involve all the students in the class as extra, different animals or they can answer in unison, as groups of each particular animal in the narrative.

Focus students' attention on words that tell where each animal is on the farm. Point out the little words, called prepositions, that show the relationship between a noun or pronoun and another word. In *Where's My Mum?* most of the prepositions tell where: *under, in, on, beside, behind, near.*

Tell students that groups of words that tell where things happen in a story are called phrases that tell where (or where phrases): *on the branch, under the tree, in the barn.* Ask students to orally suggest other 'phrases that tell where' to suit the picture of the farm in the student book. For example *in the grass, under the water, along the path.* Ask students to listen out for 'phrases that tell where' in stories you read to them.

Remind students about story maps they may have explored in narratives that they have read.

If students have trouble with question 3, they can refer to the picture on page 47 to help them decide whether the statements are facts or opinions.

Grammar Focus: Exclamations
Type of Text: Imaginative – Narrative

Student Book 2
Unit 22

The narrative *Along Came a Spider* is a spoof or send-up of the *The Little Miss Muffet* nursery rhyme. Read or recite the original rhyme to students in case they are not familiar with it. Then discuss how the narrative has been changed to make it more modern. Point out and discuss the aspects of the narrative that modernise it: the strong female character; the modern setting; the character's name; what Millie was doing when the spider appeared; the fact that Millie was not afraid of the spider; the fact that Millie was environmentally ethical – she rescued the spider and did not kill it.

Focus students' attention on the punctuation in *Along Came a Spider:* the statements, questions, and particularly the exclamations, and the punctuation marks for each. Also point out the speech marks that indicate what is actually said by Millie Muffet. Have two students act out the tale for the class. One student can play Millie and say all her lines, and the other student can be the narrator and say the remaining text.

Ask your school's teacher/librarian for examples of fairytales and nursery rhymes that have been parodied. Read them to the class. Divide the class into groups and have them organise performances of a nursery rhyme or fairytale of their choice. They can perform an original version or a spoof, or they can create their own modern version of a tale.

Have students perform for the class. Discuss any differences in the way they presented the tales and the traditional versions.

Grammar Focus: Emotive words
Type of Text: Persuasive – Advertisement

Student Book 2
Unit 23

Llamas for Sale! is an advertisement for llamas. The function of advertisements is to make people buy something. Show students photos or illustrations of llamas. Point out the spelling of *llamas*, with the double l.

Discuss these aspects of grammar in *Llamas for Sale!*:

- noun groups with adjectives *(fabulous offer)*
- statements, exclamations and questions
- emotive words to appeal to people's emotions *(You must buy now! This fabulous offer is for today only.)*
- high modality *(don't miss out!)*

Ask students if they have noticed the term *not sold separately* in advertisements. Ask why they think the llamas would not be sold separately. The answer is that llamas are very sociable and need to be with other llamas.

Ask students about their favourite television advertisements and what the advertisements are for. Ask them what they like about the advertisements and if there is anything about the ads that annoys them.

Choose a classroom item such as an IWB, a cupboard, or a textbook and ask students to suggest emotive words, adjectives and phrases that would convince people to buy that item. Make a list of their suggestions. Ask for a volunteer to choose a classroom item and try to 'sell' it to the class. Use some of the words and phrases and sing them to a familiar tune to create an advertising jingle.

Remind students of the difference between fact and opinion and then look at the list of sales words. Ask students which were fact and which were opinion.

Display and discuss students' advertisements written for the **Try it yourself!** activity. Conduct a class vote for the most successful advertisement.

Grammar Focus: Reported speech
Type of Text: Persuasive – Discussion

Student Book 2
Unit 25

The discussion *Zoos* in Unit 25 presents different points of view about zoos. Read the text to students and point out: the orientation, which includes a question; the words used to introduce the different opinions *(Some people, Other people)*; and the summing-up statement or conclusion, which gives the author's own opinion.

Ask students their opinions about zoos. Make sure they give reasons for their opinions.

Tell students that the four parts of the text *Zoos* (orientation, first opinion with reasons, second opinion with reasons, and conclusion) are written as four paragraphs. Teach them the concept that a paragraph consists of one or more sentences based on the same idea, or the same aspect of the topic. Paragraphs begin on new lines. Examine some paragraphs in factual Big Books or narratives.

The *Zoos* text reports what people believe or think. When writers report what people have said they do not need to use speech marks, as in the sentence: *Other people say that zoos do an important job.* This way of recording what was said is called reported speech. It is speech that is not quoted in speech marks. Show students examples of quoted and reported speech.

Reported speech: *Ping said that she likes meerkats.*

Quoted speech: *Ping said, "I like meerkats."*

Have students work in pairs. Have them tell each other what they had for breakfast. Then have each student report what their partner had for breakfast to another pair as reported speech.

Amira said that she had pancakes and orange juice for breakfast.

Students could take turns to write the reported speech on a chart.

Read picture book narratives to the class and point out examples of quoted and reported speech.

Grammar Focus: Noun groups
Type of Text: Informative – Explanation

Student Book 2
Unit 26

Point out to students that the text *How Do Baby Penguins Eat?* is an explanation. It explains the process involved in feeding penguin chicks. Point out to students that explanations are often accompanied by visual elements such as flow diagrams, cycle diagrams, photos and illustrations. Display explanation texts, books and posters available in your school for students to examine.

Point out the structure of the explanation *How Do Baby Penguins Eat?*: the orientation and then the examples numbered 1, 2 and 3 to indicate the three ways different penguin species feed their babies. The process of feeding is explained using the connective *then*, which links through time. More sophisticated explanations in scientific journals would include more complex use of connectives to link ideas through cause and effect. Have students create diagrams to show the three ways that baby penguins can eat.

Revise with students the functions of different words in the noun group:

- describing adjectives: *fishy food, rich oil*
- number adjectives: *three ways, many birds*
- classifying adjectives: *baby penguins, pet bird, penguin's stomach.*

Extend students' understanding of noun groups to include words that:

- point out: *that book, this desk, a penguin, the parent*
- show possession: *their chicks, penguin's stomach.*

Words that show possession include:

- *his, her, their, my, our, its, your*
- nouns that use an apostrophe to show possession: *Matilda's toe; Duncan's teeth.*

Grammar Focus: Time words and word groups
Type of Text: Informative – Recount

Student Book 2
Unit 27

Reptile Encounter is a recount of events on a class excursion. Read the text with students. Remind students that recounts tell about events that have already occurred, in a time sequence. Remind students of the function of time words in texts to help sequence events. Time words include days of the week, months and words such as *then, after, before, lastly* as well as phrases such as *in the morning, during the storm, after the rain, at lunchtime*.

Review noun groups as groups of words with a main noun, and words that tell more about the main noun. Ask students to suggest words to describe nouns in ever-expanding rows. For example:

- *lizard*
- *blue-tongue lizard*
- *eastern blue-tongue lizard*
- *smooth-skinned eastern blue-tongue lizard*
- *snail-eating, smooth-skinned eastern blue-tongue lizard*
- *snail-eating, four-legged, smooth-skinned eastern blue-tongue lizard*

You could use this format to jointly construct a Dylan Thomas portrait (see page 18 for instructions on Dylan Thomas portraits).

Have you ever seen an eastern blue-tongue?

Snail-eating, smooth-skinned, four-legged, Australian lizard.

Discuss and demonstrate the use of apostrophes in contractions. Tell students that to contract means to shorten. Letters are left out of contracted words and apostrophes mark the place where the missing letters were.

Jointly construct a recount with the class. Recount something that has happened in the school recently or take the students for a walk around the playground and stop at various points to look at, or listen for, something specific. Write a recount of your walk when you return to the classroom. Focus on the words that help to sequence the events in time (*first, then, after* and so on).

Grammar Focus: Alliteration, doing verbs
Type of Text: Informative – Procedure/Recipe

Student Book 2
Unit 28

Read the *'Talk to the Animals' Potion* with students. Discuss the function and structure of recipes with students. Point out the goal (given in the heading of the recipe), the list of ingredients needed and the Method – a series of steps written in number order. Also point out the warnings accompanying the recipe. Display recipe books and other examples of instruction texts for students to examine.

Students have been introduced to commands in earlier units. Ask students what they notice about the wording in the Method list. They should notice that the doing verb is at the start of each command *(grind, mix, apply, leave, dance, chant, rinse)*. Have all students dance and chant as instructed by the recipe.

Alliteration is about repeated sounds at the beginning of words: *cha-cha, chant; ling-gwistic ling-gwini la la; flamingo feathers; thimbles of thistle; pink petunia petals; cups cow cream.*

Create some class tongue twisters that make use of alliteration. Illustrate and display the tongue twisters. Have students practise saying them as quickly as they can without getting tongue-tied. Read picture books and poems that make use of alliteration.

Explain the play on words in *ling-gwistic ling-gwini la la*. Linguistics is the study of the sounds, words and grammar of language. *Lingo* is a colloquial term for language. *Lingua* (pronounced *lingwa*) means tongue. Linguine is a type of flat thin pasta. *Linguine* means 'little tongues' in Italian. So the chant is a play on words about getting tongue-tied like spaghetti with language. Have students create portraits to illustrate 'tongue-tied'.

Question 5 asks students to write the two rhyming words in *'Talk to the Animals' Potion: lotion* and *ocean.*

Grammar Focus: Phrases
Type of Text: Informative – Information report

Student Book 2 **Unit 29**

Read *Ringtail Possums* with students. Discuss the information about possums in the text. Discuss the meanings of some of the technical terms used, such as *marsupial, underbelly, threatened by loss of habitat* and so on. Point out that informative texts often include technical terms about the subject matter.

Show students a map of Australia and the location of the peppermint gum forests in the south-west of Western Australia where this possum lives. Extra information is available on the internet.

Point out that information reports usually have categories of information. Ask students to suggest headings for the categories of information given about the possum, for example:

What it is

Where it lives

What it looks like

What it does/its behaviour

What it eats

What problems it faces

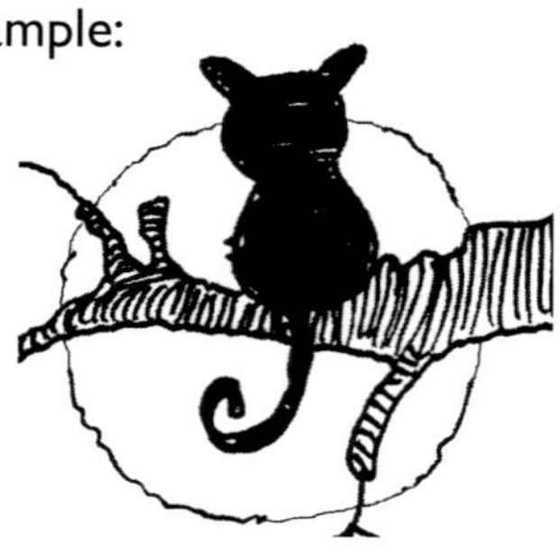

Students have dealt with words and word groups that tell where or when in earlier units. This unit expands on this understanding of prepositional phrases. A phrase is described as a group of words that go together. Lots of phrases start with prepositions. Remind students that prepositions are the little words that come before a noun or pronoun to show how one thing relates to another. Prepositions include: *in, at, without, by, for, along, below.* Make a class chart of prepositions.

Prepositional phrases start with a preposition and can tell:

where: in the garden, under the blanket, on the donkey

when: before dinner, after lunch, during library time

with whom: without us, with Aunty Laura, with Tom and Violet

why: because of the rain

with what: with a net, with sunscreen, with prickles and spikes

Grammar Focus: Word chains
Type of Text: Informative – Information report

Student Book 2 **Unit 31**

Read *Corroboree Frogs* with students. Discuss the information about the frogs in the text. Discuss the meanings of some of the technical terms used, such as *extinct, froglets, hatch* and so on. Remind students that information reports usually have categories of information. Ask students to suggest headings for the categories of information given about the frogs, for example:

What it is

Where it lives

What it looks like

What it does/its behaviour

Ask students what else they would like to know about the corroboree frog. Have students research for further information to find out, for example:

What it eats

What eats it

What problems it faces for survival

Show students a map of Australia and the location of the Snowy Mountains in New South Wales, where the corroboree frog lives. Extra information such as the effect of climate change on the frog is available on the internet.

The unit deals with word chains (lexical chains). They are the chains of content words that link content strands in a text. A text about frogs will include words for frogs and frog behaviour. Lexical chains can include nouns, verbs and phrases. A lexical chain differs from a reference chain. A reference chain only includes nouns and the words used to refer to these nouns. For example:

Reference chain: *The southern corroboree frog, it, they, frogs.*

Lexical chain: *The southern corroboree frog, almost extinct, yellow stripes on a black body, adult frogs.*

It is useful for students to recognise how words in a text about frogs will all relate in some way to an aspect of a frog's life. This understanding will help students 'stick to the topic' or 'stay on topic' when creating their own information reports and other texts.

Grammar Focus: Tense
Type of Text: Imaginative – Narrative/Fable

Student Book 2 **Unit 32**

Discuss fables with students. A fable is a narrative that has a message or a moral. Fables are used to teach lessons. Share fables from a variety of cultures and countries with students. Discuss the lesson taught in each.

Have students create comic strips to illustrate a fable of their choice.

Have students work in groups to dramatise a fable of their choice.

The Chimp and the Crocodile is based on Aesop's fable about the lion and the mouse. Its moral is 'One good turn deserves another'. An alternative moral for this fable, in some references, is 'Little friends may make great friends'. It does not particularly matter the exact wording of the moral you use, as long as students recognise a moral in a fable.

Discuss the concept of tense with students. Tense is the way a verb is written to tell whether the events are happening now, happened in the past or will happen in the future. For example:

past (has happened already): *I ate.* *He ran.* *She jumped.*

present (is currently happening or happens on an ongoing basis): *I am jumping.* *Frogs jump.*

future (will happen in the future): *I will jump.*

An understanding of tense is important for students to maintain consistency in the time frames that they are speaking or writing about. For example, recounts use past tense verb forms and information reports use present tense because they deal with the way things are. Also, ESL students might have difficulty with the forms of some verbs such as the verb *to go*, which changes form as follows:

I went. → *I am going.* → *I will go.*

Students might say, for example, I *goed* for past tense.

Another common problem with tense is with the verb *bring*, which changes form as follows:

I brought. → *I am bringing.* → *I will bring.*

Students might say *bringed, brung, branged* or similar for past tense.

Grammar Focus: Sentences
Type of Text: Informative – Procedure/Instructions

Student Book 2 **Unit 33**

Read the instructions *How to Look After a Tarantula* to the class. Ask whether students have a pet tarantula or have heard of a tarantula as a pet. Brainstorm the needs of a pet: food, water, shelter, exercise, stimulation. Discuss the steps in the instructions that relate to these issues.

Discuss the structure and features of the text *How to Look After a Tarantula.* It starts with a statement of goal (the title). It lists the tarantula's needs and describes how to meet them.

Have students do further research about tarantulas. They could work in groups to write an explanation for how tarantulas moult. They could write an information report about a particular kind of tarantula and where it comes from in the wild. They could write an exposition text to present a point of view about keeping a tarantula as a pet or an exposition to convince others that the tarantula is the best pet to have. They could also create an advertisement for print media or television to sell tarantulas.

Allow students to form their own groups or allocate students to mixed-ability groups.

Revise sentences with students. Use sentence cloze activities where sentences are scrambled and students need to organise the words or word groups into the correct sequence. **Reproducible 3** (page 77) can be used in a sentence cloze activity – just cut out each sentence, and then cut the sentences into separate words or word groups and have students organise the words into sentences. Remind students of the difference between sentences that state information or opinion (statements), sentences that ask questions (questions), and sentences that exclaim something in surprise or anger (exclamations).

Grammar Focus: Joining sentences
Type of Text: Informative – Explanation

Student Book 2
Unit 34

How Sea Animals Breathe is an explanation text. Read the text to students and then ask for volunteers to explain in their own words how whales and fish breathe, summarising or paraphrasing to show they comprehend the meanings in the explanation.

Ask students what they notice about the structure and the features of the text. It begins with an orientation or introduction, which states that whales are mammals, and then it tells in detail how whales breathe air. The explanation is written in a sequence that shows one thing leads to the next. The second paragraph explains how fish breathe. This is also written in a sequence that demonstrates one step at a time of the explanation.

Talk to students about the sequence and how important it is to sequence an explanation accurately. Jigsaw cloze is a useful activity to use with explanations to assist students to understand the importance of logical order (see page 13 for instructions on jigsaw cloze).

Explanations often make use of connectives. They connect parts of a sentence in a meaningful way. Connectives, including conjunctions, link ideas through a text by:

- adding information *in addition* *as well as*
- comparing things *if* *however* *despite*
- showing one thing causes another *unless* *therefore* *so*
- showing a time sequence *then* *next*
- sequencing arguments *firstly* *finally* *secondly*

In these early stages, students will probably only deal with simple explanations. The easiest connectives for students to recognise and make use of in their own texts are those that add information and those that show a time sequence. More sophisticated explanations in scientific journals, for example, would include more complex use of connectives to link ideas through cause, comparison or contrast.

Point out to students that explanations are often accompanied by visual elements such as flow diagrams, cycle diagrams, photos and illustrations. Display any explanation texts, books and posters available in your school for students to examine.

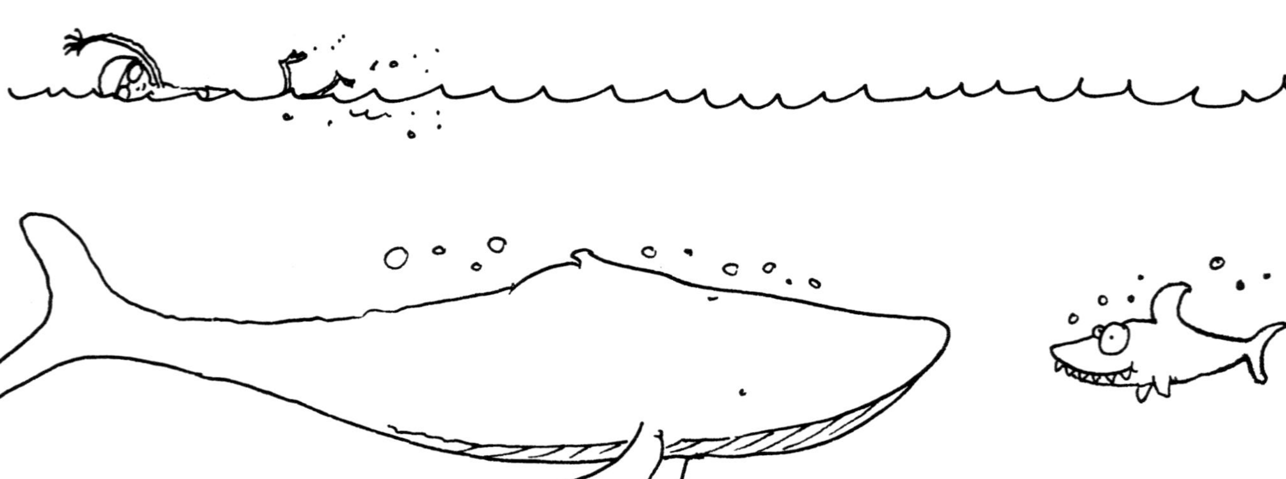

see page 13

Name ______________________ **Date** ______________________

Write a doing verb from the box on each line.

eats	spins	grows	sheds
crawls	grows	changes	

A tiny silkworm larva hatches from its egg. The larva ____________ mulberry leaves and ____________ bigger and bigger. As it ____________ bigger it ____________ its skin a number of times. When the larva has grown big enough it ____________ a cocoon around itself. Inside the cocoon the larva ____________ into a pupa. Then, after a few weeks, a moth ____________ out of the cocoon.

see page 13

Name ______________________ **Date** ______________

Write a pronoun from the box on each line.

I	me	me	she	we
She	we	me	me	We

At the Playground

Yesterday Mira took __________ to the playground. Mira is my neighbour.

First __________ played on the seesaw. Then Mira watched __________ on the slippery dip.

After that __________ pushed __________ on the swing.

__________ pushed __________ really high.

__________ threw the ball to Mira's dog for a while before __________ went home.

__________ had great fun at the playground.

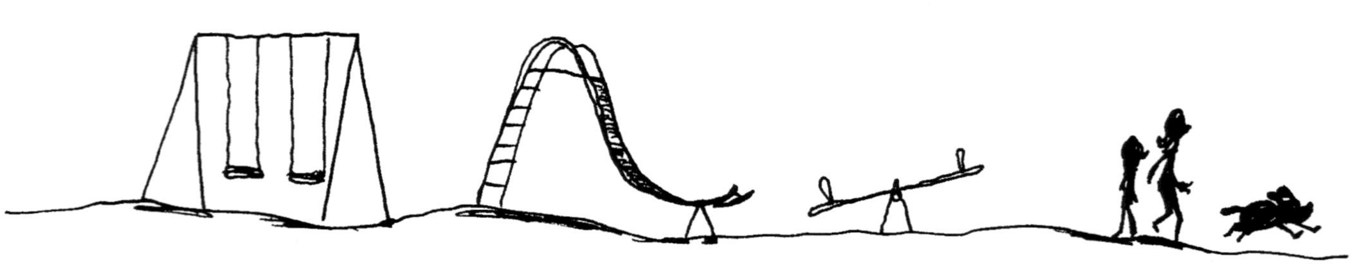

see page 13

A Moreton Bay Fig Tree

The tree in our school playground is a Moreton Bay fig tree.

It has a thick trunk and thick branches.

I love the way its twisty roots stick up above the ground.

It's really old.

My teacher thinks it is at least one hundred years old.

It gives birds and insects a place to live.

It gives us shade all year round.

I eat my lunch under its canopy every day.

It's a beautiful tree.

see page 15

Name ______________________ **Date** ______________

Check all the verbs. Cross out the incorrect verbs. Write the correct verbs.

Sloths ~~is~~ *are* mammals. They lives in South America. Sloths are mostly brown fur. Sloths mainly ate leaves but sometimes they ate insects and lizards. Sloths are ate by jaguars. Sloths sleeping for at least fifteen hours every day. They spent a lot of time laying around in trees where they is hidden from view. When they were on the ground they walking very, very slowly. In fact, sloths were probably the slowest animals on earth.

Grammar Rules! Teacher Resource Book 1–2 (ISBN 978 1 4202 3663 7) © Tanya Gibb/Macmillan Education Australia 2016

see page 15

Freeze Frame: ______________________________

Scene: ______________________________

____

Scene: ______________________________

____

Scene: ______________________________

____

Scene: ______________________________

____

Freeze Frame: ______________________________

Scene: ______________________________

____

Scene: ______________________________

____

Scene: ______________________________

____

Scene: ______________________________

____

VERB/ADVERB IMPROVISATIONS

see page 16

Verb	Adverb
talk	excitedly
complain	loudly
hide	carefully
sneak	quietly
write	slowly
type	quickly
eat	hungrily
argue	angrily
smile	happily
cheer	noisily

see page 15

Freeze Frame: ______________________________

Scene: ______________________________

____

Scene: ______________________________

____

Scene: ______________________________

____

Scene: ______________________________

____

Freeze Frame: ______________________________

Scene: ______________________________

____

Scene: ______________________________

____

Scene: ______________________________

____

Scene: ______________________________

____

see page 16

Proper noun	Common noun	Adjective	Verb

see page 16

Name ______________________ **Date** ______________

Find these doing verbs.

jumped	hopped	skipped	ate	saw	looked
wrote	swam	sat	sank	winked	danced

The words may be horizontal →
vertical ↑ ↓
or backwards ←

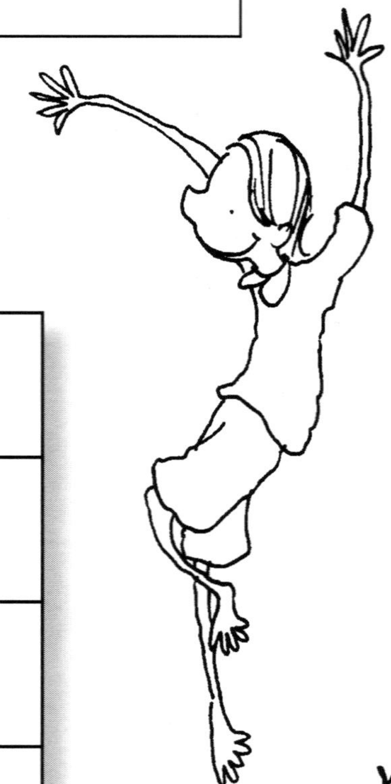

j	u	m	p	e	d
d	p	a	w	a	s
e	e	w	i	o	k
k	d	s	u	w	i
n	e	a	m	r	p
i	k	n	z	o	p
w	o	k	a	t	e
h	o	p	p	e	d
j	l	s	a	t	h
d	a	n	c	e	d

see page 16

noun fruit		noun teeth	
noun pet		noun car	
noun book		noun tree	
noun shoe		noun flower	
noun scissors		noun spider	

Name ______________________ **Date** ______________

Write an exclamation in each speech balloon. Remember to use exclamation marks.

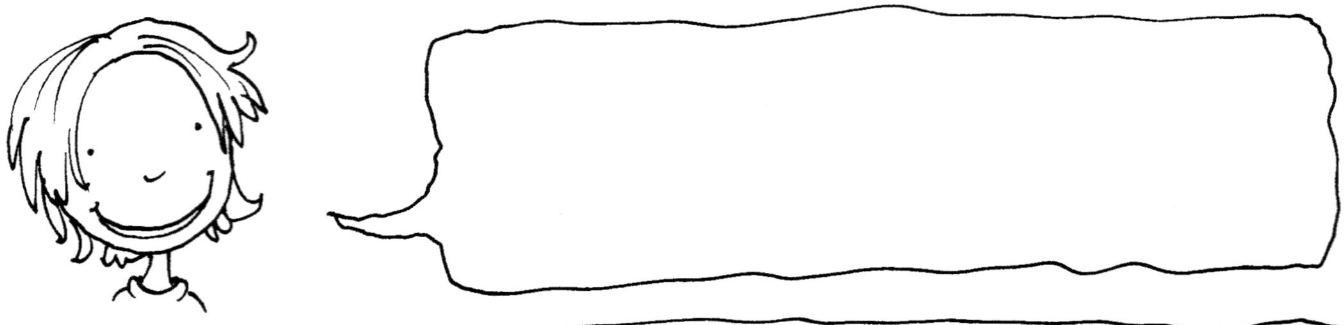

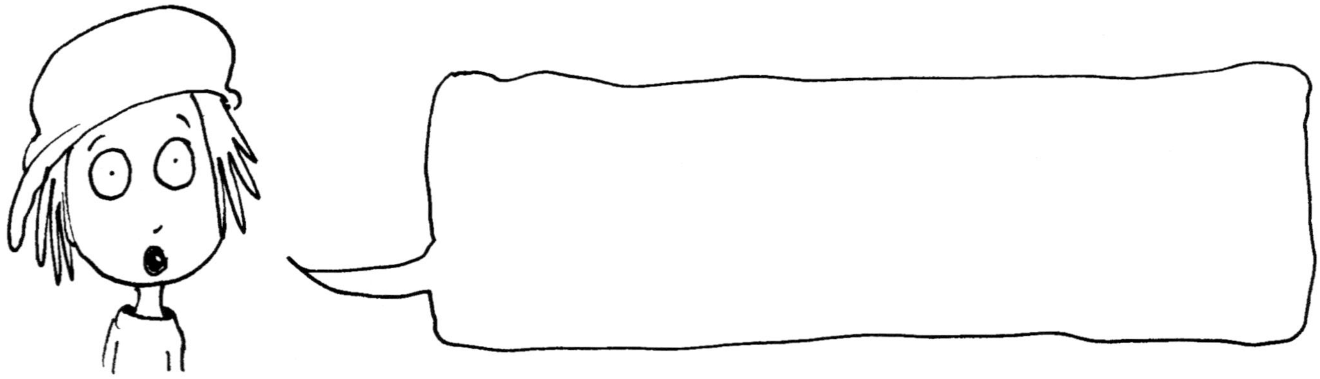

Draw a person's face in the box.

Write an exclamation for the person to say. Use speech marks and a saying verb.

____

____

____

____

____

Grammar Rules! Teacher Resource Book 1–2 (ISBN 978 1 4202 3663 7) © Tanya Gibb/Macmillan Education Australia 2016

Name

	Concept	Date	Comment Evaluation/Follow-up
Clause to whole text level	**Fact and opinion** **Sentences** Statement Question Command Exclamation		
	Quoted speech		
	Personal pronouns		
	Reported speech		
	Cohesion through repetition		
	Logical order		
	Conjunctions **Time connectives**		
Word and word group level	**Nouns** Proper Common Compound words Single and plural nouns		
	Adjectives		
	Verbs Doing Saying Thinking and feeling **Contractions**		
	Adverbs and phrases How words Where phrases Time words		

Name

	Concept	Date	Comment Evaluation/Follow-up
Clause to whole text level	**Paragraphs**		
	Fact and opinion		
	Sentences		
	Statement		
	Question		
	Command		
	Exclamation		
	Quoted and reported speech		
	Personal pronouns		
	Lexical chains		
	Connectives		
Word and word group level	**Nouns**		
	Proper nouns		
	Common nouns		
	Compound words		
	Single and plural nouns		
	Ownership		
	Adjectives		
	Verbs		
	Doing		
	Saying		
	Thinking and feeling		
	Being and having		
	Tense		
	Contractions		
	Adverbs		
	Adverbial phrases		
	Prepositional phrases		
	How, when, where		

Merit Certificate

Congratulations!

Name ______________________________

For working constructively with others on grammar tasks.

Signed ______________________ Date ____________

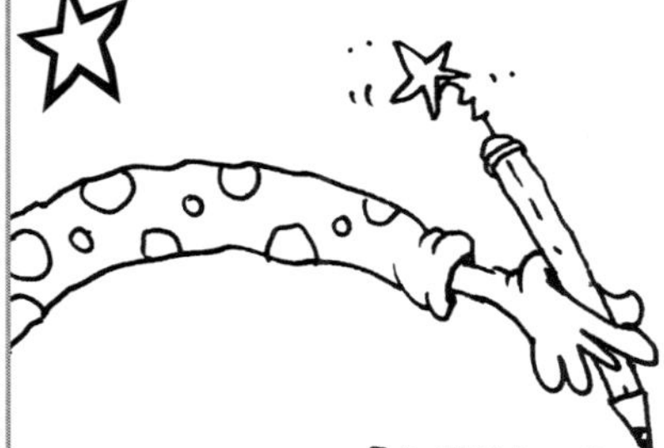

Merit Certificate

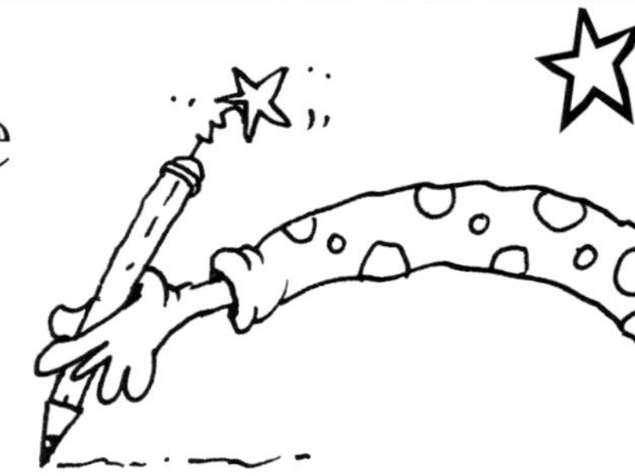

Awarded to:

Name ______________________________

For USING grammar to improve your writing.
A fabulous effort!

Signed ______________________ Date ____________

Merit Certificate

Congratulations!

Name ______________________________

Great sequencing of information in factual texts.

Signed ______________________ Date ____________

Merit Certificate

Wow!

Name ______________________________

For using grammar to write interesting stories.

Keep up the great work!

Signed ______________________ Date ____________

Student Book 1 Answers

Unit 1

2 bird, frog, bee, dog, ball, bird
3 worm, beetle, leaf, dirt, rock, hose, bucket
4 wishing well, giant, elf, fairy, ogre, castle, frog, swan
5 Answers will vary.

Unit 2

1 fish, mouth/tail, eyes, fins/gills
2 tank, friend, shell, water
3 cat, dog, rabbit, bird
4 fish → tank
rabbit → hutch
cat → basket
dog → kennel
bird → cage
5 Answers will vary.

Unit 3

1 Answers will vary.
2 Answers will vary.
3 Answers will vary.
4 apple, watermelon, cat food, banana
5 Answers will vary.
6 sausages, beans, broccoli, bread, potatoes (Answers may vary.)
7 Answers will vary.
8 Answers will vary. For example: cereal, fruit, toast, bread, cheese, rice

Unit 4

1 Robert, Claire, Joe, Marie
2 Jilly, Tiger, David, Tim
3 Answers will vary.
4 Answers will vary.
5 Answers will vary.
6 Answers will vary. For example: Tommy/Terry, Digger/Woofie, Sally/Sam, Fluffy/Snowy
7 Answers will vary.

Unit 5

1 Monday, Tuesday, Wednesday, Thursday, Friday, Saturday, Sunday
2 Answers will vary if students write about their own day. For example: Wednesday, sunny
3 hot, rainy, windy, cloudy, cold, foggy, sunny
4 brown, blue, happy/tall, tall/happy
5 sunny, rainy, cloudy, windy
6 jumper, scarf, beanie, jacket

Unit 6

1 dog, picnic, bird, tree, flower, grass
2 sunny, good, pretty, happy
3 month → October
day → Wednesday
boy → Fred
girl → Abby
cat → Tabby
4 Saturday, Sunday
5 Sooty, Tom, Sally, Bethany
7 brown, blue, red, big
8 sad, small, spotty, yellow
9 Answers will vary.

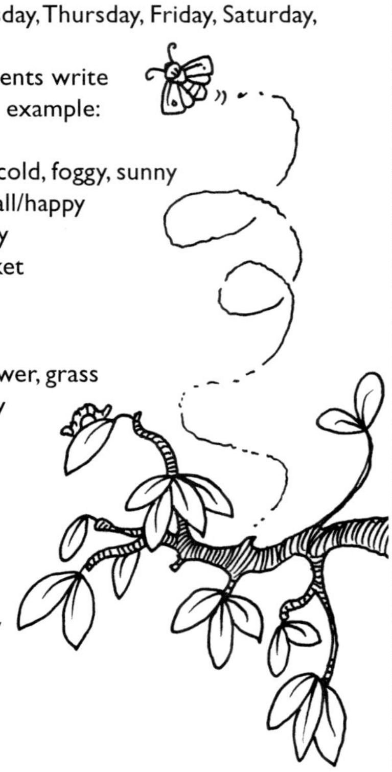

Unit 7

2 milk, eggs, wool, apples
4 Walk → to the start.
Jump → over the fence.
Eat → an apple.
Gallop → to the finish.
Drink → some water.
5 Answers will vary. For example:
I can ride a tractor. I can play in the barn.

Unit 8

1 seesaw, slippery dip, swing
2 threw, chased, climbed, pushed, went
3 eat, chase, sleep, run, swim, scratch, beg
4 fry, chop, mix, grill, bake
5 draw, paint, write, scratch, chop
6 The cat is sleeping. The frog is jumping.

Unit 9

1 Work, Raise, Listen, Look, Keep, Walk
2 Answers will vary. For example: Don't walk with scissors. Share with others. Play nicely. Don't annoy other people. Sit properly on your chair.
3 Answers will vary. For example: Tidy your room. Eat your dinner.
4 Answers will vary. For example: Don't talk with your mouth full. Don't spit your food. Eat nicely.; Clean up the mess. Take the dog outside.
5 Answers will vary.
6 Answers will vary.
7 Stop!, Help!, Run!

Unit 10

1 This morning, Firstly, Then, After
2 thirdly, firstly, secondly, finally
3 firefighter → puts out fires
dentist → looks after your teeth
ambulance officer → helps if you are hurt in an accident
police officer → helps to keep you safe
teacher → teaches you things
4 1: in the morning
2: during lunch
5: at bedtime
3: after lunch
4: before dinner
5 morning, night, afternoon, daytime, sunrise
6 vet, dentist, coach, nurse

Unit 11

1 sick, dull
2 Elvis
3 Last week, while
4 said, asked
5 yelled/giggled, whispered, asked, yelled/giggled, told
6 whispered, chuckled, giggled, cried, announced, yelled
7 cheeped → bird
clucked → chicken
mooed → cow
neighed → horse
brayed → donkey
8 quacked, woofed, snorted, growled

Unit 12

1 Answers will vary. For example: Sit!, Jump!, Fetch!
2 Answers will vary. For example: Wash the paintbrushes. Wash the dishes. Tidy the room. Tidy the cupboard.
3 shark → swims
kangaroo → jumps
monkey → swings
snake → slithers
bird → flies
4 desk, teacher, chair, hat, book
5 Answers will vary. For example: run, leap, jump, hop, kick, bend, stretch, stomp, dance, skip
6 Answers will vary. For example: My legs are long and straight.
7 3: After breakfast I cleaned my teeth.
1: This morning I woke at 7 o'clock.
2: Then I had breakfast.
4: After that I got dressed.
5: Then I came to school.
8 gobble gobbled → turkey
croaked → frog
hissed → snake
grunted → pig
neighed → horse
9 NO!, Wow!, Hurray!
10 laughed, asked, croaked, howled, ordered

Unit 13

1 tree, playground, trunk, branches, roots, ground, teacher, years, birds, insects, place, shade, year, lunch, canopy, day, tree. **Note:** Students may also underline school in 'school playground', although this is technically an adjective in this case as it tells what kind of playground.
2 Moreton Bay
3 thick, twisty, old, beautiful
4 Ben ate → two bananas.
Min held → my hand.
George washed → the car.
Fiona crossed → the road.
5 Dad cooked pancakes.
My brother got a haircut.
The clown was silly.
The dog chased seagulls.
6 The tree is tall. It has strong branches. It is a gum tree.
7 Sit under the tree. Eat your lunch. Place your rubbish in the bin. Put away your lunch box.
8 Answers will vary. For example: Sit down to eat. Eat your sandwiches. Pack away your lunch box. Put your rubbish in the bin.

Unit 14

1 Questions: What do moths study in school? Why is six afraid of seven? Who's there? Boo who?
2 Answers will vary.
3 Answers will vary.
4 Answers will vary. For example: Do you trust me? Are you a good shot?
5 full stop, question mark, question mark, full stop

Unit 15

1 cats, birds, snakes, girls, boys
2 dresses, peaches, boxes
3 fish, children, flies, loaves, teeth
4 4 ducks, 3 shoes, 3 butterflies
6 Answers will vary. For example: fly, hop, walk, sleep, eat, sit, watch, look
7 Answers will vary.
8 Answers will vary.

Unit 16

1 beautiful, turquoise, blue, purple, long, long, crimson, fast, happy, beautiful
2 swim, eat, buy, blows
3 fins, tail, body
4 blue, purple, crimson/long, fast, tiny
5 Answers will vary.
6 fluffy → duckling
green → leaf
tall → tree
tiny → elf
cuddly → grandpa
7 Answers will vary. For example: tall, spotty, skinny, friendly, cute, beautiful
8 tiny, little, incy wincy, minuscule, petite

Unit 17

1 Paint, Colour, Cut, Hang, Make, Place
2 pens, box, paint, scissors, paper, thread, tape, glue, rocks, pebbles, fish, reeds, plants
3 Share → the chocolates.
Peel → the potatoes.
Pour → the milk.
Lick → the ice-cream.
Cut → the watermelon.
4 Lie, Chase, Jump, Roll, Run
5 Answers will vary.
6 Commands: Finish your dinner. Get a haircut. Kiss me.

Unit 18

1 Answers will vary.
2 Collect, Feed, Grow, Dive, Throw
3 read, eat, buy, wash
4 eggs, pets, books, children
6 The lion is prowling.
The bear is sleeping.
The possum is eating.
The rat is sneaking.
The shark is swimming.
7 Answers will vary. For example: What time is it? Where's my money?
8 furious, mad, cranky
9 yellow, fluffy, little

Unit 19

1 her, she
2 We
3 sleep
4 pound, lap, tummy, walls, sun, chair
5 They, he, I, She, her
6 he, she, they; him, her, them

Unit 20

1 Aunty Selma, Uncle Kenan, Lana
2 Ceric, Hastings Road, North Ryde

3 Answers will vary.
4 Answers will vary.
5 Australia, Mongo Street, Pookipoo Public School, Aunty Tilly, Uncle Bing, Crazy Kids Child Care Centre, New Zealand
7 house, aquarium
8 Answers will vary. For example: shark, stingray, octopus
9 Students to colour the sea star, octopus, sea jelly, stingray and shark

Unit 21

1 6
2 Follow the path. I will buy a sandwich. Laura has a new watch.
3 What day is it? → Today is Tuesday.
Who wants pizza? → We all want pizza.
Where are you going? → I'm going to the library.
What's for dinner? → We're having stir-fry for dinner.
Will it rain today? I don't think it will rain today.
4 Answers will vary.
5 Answers will vary.
6 Answers will vary.

Unit 22

1 because, and, so
2 The dragon lived alone; needed a friend.
3 Answers will vary.
4 but, because, so, and
5 because, and, so, but
6 all the way to China; a friend; to the mountain top; happily ever after.

Unit 23

1 4: The milk is cooled.
5: The milk is bottled.
3: The milk is heated.
2: The milk goes to the factory.
6: The milk goes to the shop.
1: The milk is pumped out of the cow.
2 fact, opinion, fact, fact, opinion, fact
3 Cows are females. Bulls are males. Baby cows suck milk from udders. Baby cows are called calves.
4 milked, they, drink, milk, make
5 Answers will vary. For example: how, now, Wow, pow; pay, hay, may, ray

Unit 24

1 Answers will vary. For example: bad, dad; peep, sheep; dent, sent; pound, sound
2 What did you eat for dinner? → I ate sushi for dinner.
Where did you put the scissors? → I put the scissors in the cupboard.
Why did you buy a cockatiel? → I bought a cockatiel because it can talk.
3 they, he, she, you
4 you, us, me, he, she, it, them, they
5 Kylie lives in Perth.
Eddie lives on Baker Street in Mildura.
Aunty Maggie lives in Dunedoo.
6 opinion, fact, fact, fact, opinion
7 Answers will vary.
8 and, but, because, so

Unit 25

1 Answers may vary. For example: yesterday, now, tomorrow, later, soon
2 Once upon a time, One day
3 I have a sandwich and an apple → at lunchtime.
I have a banana on toast → in the morning.
I have noodles and vegetables → at dinnertime.
4 swished, swooshed, smashed, crashed
5 Splat, Boom, Snuffle thud, Chug chug chug

Unit 26

1 Slurpy Slime Shake
2 green, good
3 Answers will vary.
4 Slurpy Slime Shake
Answers will vary. For example: Sweet, Slippery
5 Answers will vary. For example: Terry, Tony's, Lisa
6 Answers will vary. For example: Dizzy, dangerous, Sassy, sweet
7 you'll, it's
8 You'll, I'll, She's It's
9 can't → cannot
don't → do not
isn't → is not
didn't → did not
10 Answers will vary.

Unit 27

1 think, believe, want to kill, shouldn't hate, love
2 feels, think, love, like, hope, want, imagine
3 Answers will vary.
4 harmless, hate, interesting, unfair
5 hot → cold
fact → opinion
thick → thin
beautiful → ugly
live → die
6 unable, unlucky, unstuck, unlikely, unloved
7 Answers will vary.

Unit 28

1 Doing verbs: clean, mop, scrub, make, wash
Nouns: chimney, floors, toilet, beds, gowns
2 Cinderfella
3 Answers will vary.
4 Answers will vary.
5 Quietly, Spotlessly, Briskly, Neatly, Carefully
6 badly, quickly, happily, slowly, angrily, kindly
7 Answers will vary. For example: quietly/carefully/briskly, carefully/neatly, briskly, carefully
8 Answers will vary.

Unit 29

1 Two, Three, any, One, One, all, one, three, five, one, one
2 Some/Many, Many/Some, first, dozen
3 two, four, six, eight, three
4 4: Cook in oven for 30 minutes.
2: Mix ingredients well.
3: Put mixture on an oven tray.
1: Add ingredients to a large bowl.
5 Answers will vary.

Unit 30

1 5: Finally it was time to go home.
2: Then my brother did a dance.
1: Firstly the principal spoke.
3: After my brother danced, his class sang songs.
4: Eventually it was time for the last song.
2 Oink!, Baa!, Grrrowl!, Honk!, Vroom!
3 Answers will vary. For example: pretty pink, big bad
4 madly, sadly, happily, swiftly, noisily

5 he's → he is
didn't → did not
they're → they are
that's → that is
isn't → is not
you're → you are
you'll → you will
6 tall → short
up → down
give → take
finish → start
big → little
first → last
7 enjoy, understand, like, think, loved
8 four, two, many, some, one

Unit 31

1 silkworm
2 softball, bathroom, football, bedroom, Sunday, birthday
3 hatches, eats, grows, sheds, spins, changes, crawls
4 lay, eat, hatch, shed
5 3: The larva spins a cocoon.
1: A silkworm hatches from its egg.
2: The silkworm larva eats and grows bigger.
4: The moth crawls out of the cocoon.
6 moth, mouth, moth, wings

Unit 32

2 walk, turn, go, stop, follow
3 at x, along the path, across the bridge, under the bridge, at the fork, in the path, past the gingerbread house, around the tree, behind the tree, along the path, out of the well, all the way to the cottage
4 The bears waited outside their house.
The wolf hid behind the tree.
The troll hid under the bridge.
The goats walked on the grass.
Red Riding Hood strolled along the path.
5 Answers will vary.

Unit 33

1 horrible-looking
2 Answers will vary. For example: pretty, lovely, beautiful
3 What am I?
5 I really loved this story.
6 At first I thought the story was really sad.
7 "I don't believe in bunyips," said Sebastian.
"They are only in stories," commented Mum.
"I love stories about bunyips," said Sophie.
"Me too," said Sebastian.

Unit 34

1 grunt, bellow, bellow, murmur, hum
2 whisper, yell, scream, shout
3 male, female
4 8
5 5
6 grey, woolly (students may add some adjectives of their own)
7 live, climb, sleep, eat (students may add some doing verbs of their own)
8 A mammal that has a pouch for its baby.
9 Answers will vary.
10 Answers will vary.
11 Koalas, groups, fur, trees, climbers, night, leaves, noises, babies, sounds, scream

Unit 35

1 "Pick up your sock," said Dad.
"Put your schoolbag away," said Mum.
"Wash your hands," said Sara.
"You're all too bossy," said Dom.
2 unit, building, neighbours, trees, street
3 eyebrow, underwear, highway, footpath, silkworm, baseball
4 Answers will vary.
5 Answers will vary.
6 Answers will vary. For example: My toothbrush is on the sink. I can hide under my bed. A bird sleeps in a tree.
7 They, Koalas, trees, sleep, eat, make, Female, babies, koala
8 but, and, because, so

Student Book 2 Answers

Unit 1

1 The parent birds build a nest.
The mother bird lays an egg.
A chick grows inside the egg.
The chick cracks out of the egg.
The parent bird feeds the baby bird.
The young bird flies out of the nest.
2 bird, nest, egg, chick
3 nest, worm, tree, bird
4 bird, nest; worm, dirt; tree, branch; rain, water
5 eggs, nest, mother, feathers, emu

Unit 2

1 Answers will vary. For example: cake, pies, biscuits, lollies, chocolate, hot dogs
2 Answers will vary.
3 Answers will vary.
4 Answers will vary. For example: pin the tail on the donkey, pass the parcel, musical chairs
5 Tim, Marcella's, Rose Court, Mainlands, February, February
6 Monday, Tuesday, Wednesday, Thursday, Friday, Saturday, Sunday
7 Answers will vary.
8 Answers will vary.
9 Maria, Paul, Wednesday; Luca, Pixie, Tuesday; Ms Bruin, May; Big Valley State School
10 On Friday I am going to play at Kimi's house after school.
I think Roger named his new goldfish Pickle.
11 Answers will vary.
12 Answers will vary.

Unit 3

1 Frogs, Crocodiles, Owls, Snakes
2 Answers will vary. For example: Freddy frog; Christine crocodile; Oscar owl; Sandra snake
3 Answers will vary. For example: fish, turtles, whales, alligators
4 Answers will vary. For example: kangaroos, rabbits, grasshoppers, fleas
5 leap, hop, jump, swim, watch, crawl, dive, roll, swoop, fly, soar, glide, slither, slide, curl, sleep
6 a horse gallops; a camel lopes; a monkey swings; a shark prowls; a fly hovers
7 Answers will vary.
8 Answers will vary. For example: worm wriggles, lion stalks, elephant stomps, zebra runs, flea jumps, mouse scampers, eagle soars, bear prowls
9 Answers will vary.
10 digging, burrowing, tunnelling

Unit 4

1 South America
2 Answers will vary. For example: mammals, fur, leaves, insects, lizards, jaguars, trees, ground
3 eat, sleep, walk
4 eat, climb, walk, hide, sleep
5 Jaguars, Giraffes, Elephants, Sloths, Koalas
6 The sloth sleeps on the branch.
A mother sloth hugs its baby. / A baby sloth hugs its mother.
The jaguar hunts for dinner.
Sloths cannot run.

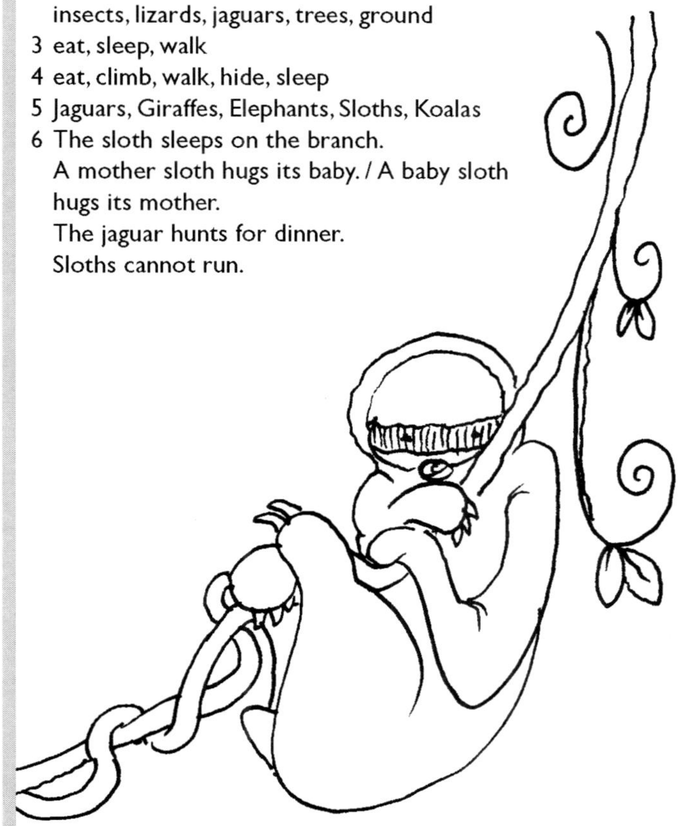

Unit 5

1 announced, said, replied, stated
2 squeaked, barked, quacked, meowed, honked
3 Bob: "I agree"; "They eat anything, even animal droppings."; "Yes, gross. Flies also vomit all the time and they vomit onto your food when they land on it. Erk!"
Jessica: "Flies have disgusting habits,"; "Yes"; "They stand anywhere they like, including on your food. They have hairs on their legs, which pick up germs and bits of other disgusting things."
4 "I don't like flies," said Hasan. "Me neither," replied Julie.
5 I just swallowed a fly!
That's gross!
6 eat, stand, vomit, land
7 Jessica, Bob

Unit 6

1 An egg is laid.
The egg hatches into a larva.
The larva grows.
The larva then goes into its pupa stage.
The adult emerges.
2 larva, egg, adult, pupa
3 Common nouns: hamster; mouse, shop, babies; possums, roof, house; beetles, legs
Proper nouns: Louie's; Mr Augustine's; Cate's; Ms Holliday
4 "Next Tuesday I am going on an excursion to the zoo," said Dean.
"Mona patted a koala," yelled Sebastian.
5 a puppy chews; a frog hops; a goat climbs; a penguin waddles; a cockroach scurries
6 Frogs croak in the pond.
Jaguars eat sloths.
Sloths have brown fur.
7 turkeys gobble; donkeys bray; lions roar; geese gobble; elephants trumpet; horses neigh; bees buzz; cats purr

Unit 7

1 sister, snake, python, skin, silk, pet
2 Molly
3 bite/bitten
4 Answers may vary. For example: slide, slither, bite, squeeze
5 older sister, brown splotches, soft/smooth skin, great pet, beautiful snake, gentle/placid snake
6 warm, active, placid/gentle
7 tiny, heavy, sleepy, toothy, tall
8 Answers will vary. For example: The dog is eating.
9 smooth, brown, quiet, soft

Unit 8

1 mice, pets, wheel, toys, house, apartment, home
2 cute, entertaining, fun, small, cheap, best
3 Answers will vary. For example: run, play, eat, sleep, exercise, chew
4 hope, want, thinks, feel
5 think, believe
6 worry, wonder, love, need, concentrate, like, dislike
7 Answers will vary.
8 Answers will vary.
9 tall, short; thin, thick; rough, smooth; loud, quiet
10 hate, agree, believe, like

Unit 9

1 Gran, Pa, Mum, Dad, Midnight, Sundance, Sara
2 shop, puppy, dogs, goldfish, pets, tank, gravel, bridge, fish, plants
3 asked, said, says
4 Answers will vary. For example: Sara loves her goldfish.
5 Answers will vary. For example: "Thank you for my goldfish," said Sara.
6 First, then, Finally
7 I asked Mum for a puppy but she said that dogs make Dad sneeze. So we decided that goldfish were the best pets for us.
8 because, unless, Since
9 4; 2; 1; 3

Unit 10

1 wings, baskets, stinger, head, legs
2 are, have, has, am, was
3 Bees make honey.
Only female bees have stingers.
Tube-tongues are good for sucking nectar.

Unit 11

1 Common nouns: dinosaur, family, mountain, mountain, elders, creatures, morning, nest, sound, branches, pterodactyl, predator, nest, egg, brother, sister, egg, edge, cliff, egg, mountain, swamp
Proper noun: Freddy
2 beautiful, terrifying, huge, gigantic, dingy
3 Egg: slipped, rolled
Freddy: woke, looked, ran, watched
4 Answers will vary. For example: worried (that he'd be eaten), hoped (that he was safe)
5 Whoosh, Crash
6 snap, thump, sizzled, popped
7 roar → lion; whirr → fan; fizzle → drink can; purr → cat; toowit toowoo → owl
8 huge/gigantic or looked/watched
9 For example: thin: skinny, narrow; hungry: starving, famished; dozing: sleeping, napping
10 standing, below, beautiful

Unit 12

1 fluffy, smooth, hairy, fast, busy
2 Answers will vary.
3 Answers will vary. For example: sad, hot, scared, dark, low, below, off, smooth
4 so, unless, since
5 Firstly, Then, After, Finally
6 Answers will vary.
7 grunt → pig; woof → dog; hiss → snake; squeak → mouse; baa → sheep
8 good: excellent, great, terrific, wonderful, fabulous
said: stated, announced, joked, whispered, yelled

Unit 13

1 instructions, ingredient, soil, door, tree, backyard, tree, ground, bed, patch, earth, flowers, hole, worms, surface, worms, soil
3 Feed, Walk, Clean, Pick, Add
4 Answers will vary.
5 Answers will vary. For example: "Tidy your room," says Dad.
6 Answers will vary. For example: Sit! Fetch the ball.

Unit 14

1 Go out the front gate and turn right.
Cross Woodside Ave at the pedestrian crossing.
Walk along Holly Rd.
Cross Fairground St at the crossing.
Turn right down Fairground St.
The dog is at 14 Fairground St.
2 backyard; playground; shipwreck; afternoon; birthday; newspaper
3 sunglasses, footpath, football, sunlight, rainbow
4 run, chase, walk, feed, scratch, wrestle, pat, tickle, play, fetch
5 Answers will vary. For example: The dog has long, floppy ears.
6 Answers will vary. For example: "Thank you for finding my dog," said Dom.

Unit 15

1 growls, purrs, meows
2 leaps, runs, pounces, rolls, scratches, paws, licks, eats, spits
3 catnip, catnap
4 For example: herb, garden, leaf, cats
5 *It* is useful to use instead of repeating the noun all the time.
6 she; 11
7 She, them, They, It
8 Answers will vary.

Unit 16

1 Doing verbs: creep, run, knock, sit, rot, sleep
Common nouns: Cats, pads, Zebras, legs, Woodpeckers, trunks, trees, chicks, parents', feet, teeth, sweets, bed
2 For example: cats, pads, zebras, legs, woodpeckers, trees, chicks, parents, sweets
3 teeth
4 bed
5 quietly, swiftly, loudly, warmly, easily, happily
6 loudly; menacingly; madly; widely
7 Answers will vary.
8 horses, elephants, salmon, foxes, mice, ostriches

Unit 17

1 painting, painting, leopard, artist, pictures, animals, painting, leopard, branch, tree, legs, tail, branch, leopard, moment, leopard, colours, bush, leopard, painting
2 Answers will vary.
3 beautiful, relaxed, alert, brown, cream, gold, powerful
4 the painting, the leopard
5 Alan Hunt, the artist
6 wildlife, endangered
7 Siamese, huntsman, soccer, comic
8 first, many, three, few
9 two
10 dirty, oozy; sleek, grassy; hungry, juicy

Unit 18

1 Check, Run, Buy, Take, Mix
2 daylight, colour-blind, weekday, windfall, somebody
3 play, tickle, kiss, feed, scratch, pat, talk
4 She, them, He, They, It
5 bravely, slowly, cheekily
6 Answers will vary.
7 rabbits, monkeys, walruses, emus, platypuses or platypi, echidnas or echidnae
8 funnel-web, netball, crossword
9 Many, tomato; Two, Siamese; few, football; first, school

Unit 19

1 grandpa, trip, China, month, photos, visit, pandas, Chengdu, photos, pandas, Grandpa, hands, gown, gloves, doctor, pandas, germs, carrots, panda, lap, Chengdu, day, pandas
2 soft, cuddly, huge
3 Grandpa
4 giant, panda, surgical
5 Answers will vary. For example: "I think Grandpa's trip sounds fabulous," said Gina.
6 six fat piglets; three Siamese kittens; five delicious chicken sandwiches; Pete's new guinea pig
7 Billy owns <u>five goldfish</u>.
Gran collects <u>old stamps</u>.
The dog had <u>muddy feet</u>.
They have <u>photos of a beach holiday</u>.
We are moving to <u>a new house</u>.
8 Answers may vary. For example: three spotted lady beetles; two startled crabs

Unit 20

1 What kinds of animals do you look after? How do you know what to do for the animals?
2 Answers will vary.
3 Answers will vary.
4 Answers will vary.
5 Answers will vary.
6 fact, opinion, fact, opinion
7 Answers will vary.

Unit 21

1 tree, barn, branch, trough, gate, wood pile, roof, tractor
2 duckling, animals, cow, horse, cat, pig, dog, goose, chicken, turtle
3 opinion, opinion, fact, opinion, fact, fact, fact, opinion.
4 Answers may vary.
5 on, under, in, on, beside, behind, on, on, near. Students may also circle *from*, which is a preposition – but not one that tells where in this case.
6 among, between, over

Unit 22

1 Millie Muffet
2 bedroom, music, spider, ceiling, chair, door, hands
3 "Oh!";"You poor little thing! Did you hurt yourself? You don't belong in here. Let me help you."
4 Answers will vary.
5 Answers will vary.
6 her, she
7 Did you hurt yourself?
8 Oh! You poor little thing!
9 Answers will vary.
10 Answers will vary.
11 I need to clean the birdcage. statement
Sam, can you clean the birdcage? question
Can we please brush the ferret? question
Wow! exclamation
I like your ferret's crazy face. statement

Unit 23

1 beautiful brown eyes
2 A home with a good owner and a large paddock. Answers may vary.
3 and, also, as well as, so, so
4 what are you waiting for?; don't miss out!
5 and/as well as, as well as/and, also
6 beautiful, gentle, friendly, how can you resist, So what are you waiting for?, today only, fabulous offer, so don't miss out!
7 Answers will vary.
8 You <u>will love</u> these.
You <u>must</u> get one.
It's <u>very</u> friendly and lovable.
Offer <u>only on today</u>.
Intelligent and easy to train.
9 Answers will vary. For example: they are gentle and friendly; they are beautiful and gentle.

Unit 24

1 Answers will vary.
2 The llama, lovely brown eyes; The friendly llamas; Llama farms, llama wool; The scarf, soft llama wool
3 fact, opinion, opinion, fact, fact
4 Answers will vary.
5 Answers will vary.
6 Answers will vary.
7 Mum said, "I'd prefer hermit crabs."
Dad agreed, "Hermit crabs are lovely."
"I want a llama," screeched Sami.
8 Answers will vary.
9 I know you'll want one.
You must have one.
It's absolutely gorgeous.

Unit 25

1 Paragraph 1: Zoos are popular but should wild animals be kept in cages?
Paragraph 2: Zoos are cruel. Wild animals belong in the wild.
Paragraph 3: Zoos help animals survive by studying them and trying to save them.
Paragraph 4: Zoos are wonderful. They educate people about animals.
2 Kathryn said that monkeys are funny.
Eliza commented that orangutans are funnier.
Mohammed said that chimpanzees are the funniest.
3 Toby agreed, "Whales are too big for zoos."
Suri said, "I love watching the otters."
4 so, Otherwise, in case

Unit 26

1 Many birds, their chicks, three ways, baby penguins, what species, The parent, the fish, the penguin's stomach, a special chemical, the fish, A few days, the parent, the fish, the chick, The fish, The parent, their fishy food, slop, their chick's mouths, The parent, the fish, The fish, very rich oil, The parent, the chick, a pet bird, some of its food
2 the squishy old banana; A little monkey; Those monkeys; That monkey
3 my untidy cupboard, my messy bed, the jam-packed garage, my baseball, Scruff's kennel
4 their chicks, their fishy food, their chick's mouths
5 The, Whose, Which, That, What, those
6 Answers will vary.

Unit 27

1 my class, an excursion, an eastern blue tongue, a shingleback, a short round tail, its head, its favourite food, a number of different kinds of geckos, that excursion
2 It's; the apostrophe replaces the i
3 I'll → I will; he's → he is; you're → you are; we'll → we will; I'm → I am; they've → they have; could've → could have; can't → cannot
4 Last Monday, Firstly, Then, After that, Lastly
5 Last night, when, Then, tonight
6 5: <u>Then</u> it was time to go to school.
4: <u>Finally</u> I had my breakfast.
3: <u>After</u> the chickens I fed the pigs.
2: <u>Then</u> I fed the chickens.
1: <u>Firstly</u> I collected the eggs.

Unit 28

2 use, Grind, Mix, Apply, Dance, Rinse, use
3 Answers will vary. For example: mix, stir, chop, bake, fry
4 snail shell; flamingo feathers; leaves lemon; pink petunia petals; thimbles thistledown; cups cow cream; cha-cha chant; lingo ling-gwistic ling-gwini la la
5 potion, ocean
6 Answers will vary. For example: terrific, tiny tot; magnificent, muffins; daggy, dancing; potent
7 tick, thick, sick, trick; thump, clump, hump, stump; bed, red, head, fed; pickle, trickle, tickle, fickle
8 Answers will vary.

Unit 29

1 of, in, of, with, during, at, with, of, around, with, in, by, by, of
2 at, in, with, by, inside, during
3 and

4 of Western Australia; in the forest canopy; of peppermint trees; with its family; during the day; at night; with a white underbelly; of black fur; around its eyes; with a white tip; in the wild; by cats, dogs, foxes and cars; by loss; of habitat
5 tells when: during the day, at night
tells where: of Western Australia, in the forest canopy, around its eyes, in the wild
6 Answers will vary.
7 Answers will vary.

Unit 30

1 Answers will vary.
2 Selma said that she wishes she could talk to animals.
Ryan agreed that it would be great fun.
Aleisha said that she thinks they say funny things about people.
3 Pamela said, "I am worried about ringtail possums."
John said, "I'm worried too."
Riku said, "I think that foxes are the worst threat to ringtails."
4 3: After the tomato I added cheese.
4: Then I cut the sandwich in half.
1: Firstly I buttered the bread.
2: Then I put on the tomato.
5: Finally I ate the sandwich.
5 Otherwise, in case, Since, unless, so
6 the biggest slice; A beautiful butterfly; That kitten; His puppy, the puddle; her horse; your parrot
7 should've → should have; she's → she is; you'll → you will; don't → do not; I'm → I am; mustn't → must not; could've → could have
8 Answers will vary. For example: plane: lane, pane; follow: hollow; yellow: fellow, mellow; hill: pill, sill
9 Answers will vary. For example: Kane's cute cat kisses canaries. Sarah's slippery snake slithers and slides.
10 Answers will vary. For example: The polar bear hunted on the ice floes. The owl perched at the top of the tree.

Unit 31

1 The southern corroboree frog of Australia, a small area of the Snowy Mountains in New South Wales, Southern corroboree frogs, bright yellow stripes, a black body, the adult frogs, two centimetres, the tadpoles of the southern corroboree frog, back legs, front legs, their tails
2 1: The frog lays eggs.
2: The egg hatches into a tadpole.
3: The tadpole grows back legs.
4: The tadpole grows front legs and the tail disappears.
5: The froglet grows into a frog.
3 The southern corroboree frog of Australia, Southern corroboree frogs, adult frogs, frogs, tadpoles, the tadpoles of the southern corroboree frog, frogs, froglets
4 Word chain for frogs and tadpoles: Corroboree frog tadpoles; the adults; the adults
Word chain for things frogs and tadpoles eat: beetles, bugs, ants, insect larvae and mites; ants; beetles and mites
5 in a small area, of the Snowy Mountains, in New South Wales
6 are, have, am, has, is

Unit 32

1 1: One day, Charlie was playing on a branch that hung over a lake.
2: Suddenly, the branch snapped. Charlie fell into the lake.
3: A crocodile had saved his life.
4: They stayed best friends forever.
2 a small chimpanzee, the chimp's name, a branch, a lake, the branch, the lake, the deep water, the surface, a big gulp of air, A crocodile, his life, the crocodile's name, a vegetarian, her favourite food, an enormous basket of apples and other sweet fruit, the town, best friends
3 Charlie, Winifred
4 lived; snapped; lifted; saved; decided; stayed
5 fell, crawled, swam, looked

Unit 33

1 a house, a heating device, water, a small dish, food, crickets, cockroaches, moths, caterpillars
2 Answers will vary.
3 tarantulas, crickets, cockroaches, moths, caterpillars, times, backs, hours, days
4 tanks, leaves, insects, schools, children, teachers, desks, jars
5 need, be, cover, add, keep, provide, will do, eat, moult, shed, turn, moult, lie, handle, hurt, eating, feeding, bite, need, hardened
6 Tarantulas shed their exoskeletons. not a command
Cover the tank with potting mix. command
Add leaves and bark. command
Feed your tarantula crickets. command
I love my tarantula. not a command
7 Give the spider water.
Feed the spider live food.
Keep the tank warm.
Watch your tarantula moult.
Use a fish tank.

Unit 34

2 blows, breathes, dive
3 breathe, sucks, pushes
4 As
5 Because whales are mammals they need to breathe air.
Humans are mammals so they need to breathe air.
The whale breathes out used air then it breathes in fresh air.
Fish need oxygen but they don't breathe air.
Whales need to surface so that they can breathe.
Animals need oxygen otherwise they will die.
6 while, now that, after, Since

Unit 35

1 bedroom, kitchen, bathroom, lounge room, laundry
2 from its tank, in my bedroom, in the kitchen, in the bathroom, in the lounge room, in the laundry, under a wet mop
3 have, has, am, were, is
4 Answers will vary.
5 Answers will vary.
6 played, worked, mowed, helped, cooked
7 Hermit crabs swap shells. not a command
Buy extra shells for the tank. command
Touch your hermit crabs gently. command
Hermit crabs run quickly. not a command
Clean your hermit crab tank. command
8 Chickens hatch from eggs.
I have a llama.
Watch out for the spider.
The magpies are nesting.
9 Because we need milk I'll walk to the shop.
We'll take the dog too, otherwise she'll be upset.
I'll make sandwiches then I'll pack the picnic basket.
We'll take raincoats but we probably won't need them.
We'll take a blanket so that we can sit on the ground.